Vacation cabins along US 1, Maine

National Geographic's Driving Guides to America

New England

By Kay and William G. Scheller
Photographed by Shawn G. Henry
and Vincent J. Musi

Prepared by
The Book Division
National Geographic Society
Washington, D.C.

Credits

**National Geographic's
Driving Guides To America
New England**

By KAY AND WILLIAM G. SCHELLER
Photographed by SHAWN G. HENRY
and VINCENT J. MUSI

Published by
THE NATIONAL GEOGRAPHIC SOCIETY

Reg Murphy
President and Chief Executive Officer
Gilbert M. Grosvenor
Chairman of the Board
Nina D. Hoffman
Senior Vice President

Prepared by The Book Division

William R. Gray
Vice President and Director
Charles Kogod
Assistant Director
Barbara A. Payne
Editorial Director

Driving Guides to America

Elizabeth L. Newhouse
*Director of Travel Books
and Series Editor*
Cinda Rose
Art Director
Thomas B. Powell III
Illustrations Editor
Caroline Hickey, Barbara A. Noe
Senior Researchers
Carl Mehler
Map Editor and Designer

Staff for this book

Barbara A. Noe
Editor
Suez B. Kehl
Designer
Thomas B. Powell III
Illustrations Editor

Michael H. Higgins
Nancy A. Donnelly
Researchers
Carl Mehler
Map Editor and Designer

Mary Luders
Assistant Editor
Carol Bittig Lutyk
Contributing Editor

Thomas L. Gray, Joseph F. Ochlak,
Louis J. Spirito, Tracey M. Wood
Map Researchers
James Huckenpahler, Louis J. Spirito,
Martin S. Walz
Map Production
Tibor G. Tóth
Map Relief

Meredith C. Wilcox
Illustrations Assistant

Richard S. Wain
Production Project Manager
Lewis R. Bassford, Lyle Rosbotham
Production

Kevin G. Craig, Banafsheh Ghassemi,
Dale M. Herring, Peggy J. Oxford
Staff Assistants

Rick Davis
Indexer

Jennifer Emmett, Mary E. Jennings,
Joshua S. Lazarus, Andrea McQuay,
Gwen Shaffer, Thomas B. Blabey
Contributors

**Manufacturing
and Quality Management**

George V. White, *Director*
John T. Dunn, *Associate Director*
Vincent P. Ryan, *Manager*

4

Autumn along Conn. 66

Cover: Bass Head Light, Mount Desert
Island, Maine

Previous page: Lake Elmore, Vermont

Facing page: Hiking the Long Trail,
Wallingford, Vermont

Contents

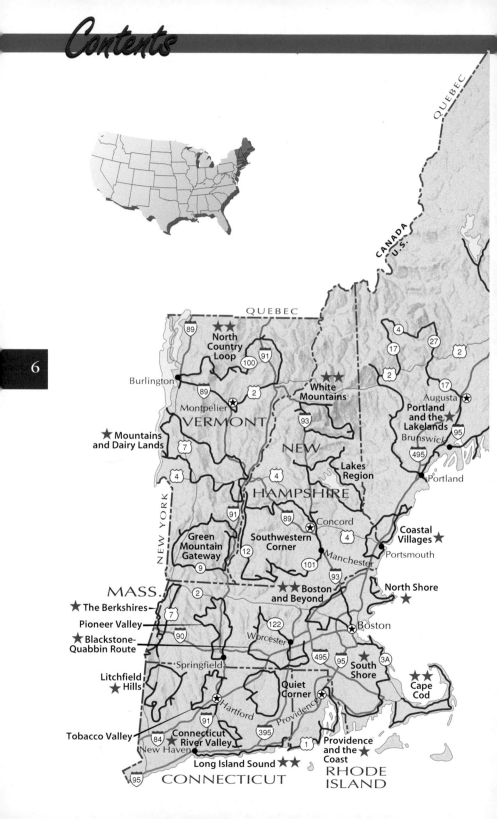

QUEBEC

CANADA
U.S.

QUEBEC

89
★★ North Country Loop
100 91
Burlington
89 2
Montpelier
VERMONT
★ Mountains and Dairy Lands
7
4
4
NEW
HAMPSHIRE
91
Green Mountain Gateway
9
12
Southwestern Corner
89 Concord
4
101
Manchester
93

93
★★ White Mountains
2
Lakes Region

4
17 27 2
2
17
Augusta ★
Portland and the Lakelands ★
Brunswick
495 95
Portland

★ Coastal Villages ★
Portsmouth

★★ Boston and Beyond
★ North Shore ★

MASS.
2
★ The Berkshires —
7
Pioneer Valley —
90
★ Blackstone-Quabbin Route
Springfield
Litchfield ★ Hills
84
Tobacco Valley —
New Haven
91
Connecticut River Valley
★ Long Island Sound ★★
95
CONNECTICUT

122
Worcester
495 95
Boston

South Shore ★
3A
★★ Cape Cod

Quiet Corner
395
Hartford
Providence
1
Providence and the Coast ★

RHODE ISLAND

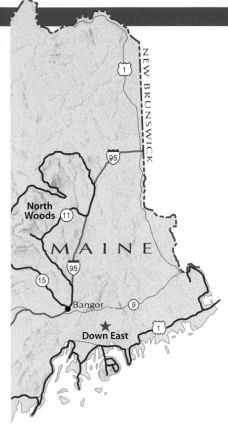

Land of Texture and Tradition 8
About the Guides 9

Maine
North Woods *10*
Down East *14*
Portland and the Lakelands *22*
Coastal Villages *28*

New Hampshire
Southwestern Corner *34*
Lakes Region *40*
White Mountains *44*

Vermont
North Country Loop *48*
Mountains and Dairy Lands *54*
Green Mountain Gateway *59*

Massachusetts
The Berkshires *64*
Pioneer Valley *70*
Blackstone-Quabbin Route *78*
Boston and Beyond *84*
North Shore *92*
South Shore *98*
Cape Cod *106*

Rhode Island
Providence and the Coast *114*

Connecticut
Long Island Sound *122*
Connecticut River Valley *130*
Quiet Corner *135*
Tobacco Valley *140*
Litchfield Hills *147*

For More Information 156
Illustrations Credits 157
Notes on Authors and Photographers 157
Index 158

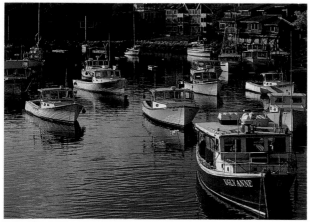

Perkins Cove, Ogunquit, Maine

· New England Character

8

Over the past four centuries, circumstance and design have created the individual characters of the New England states. Connecticut's Yankee heartland became an industrial powerhouse. Rhode Island sought its fortune through seaborne trade, and later in its factories. Massachusetts cast a beacon from its universities. Upcountry, New Hampshire wrung its textile riches from the Merrimack River. Farmers they remained in Vermont, well into our own time. And Maine still lives its separate lives, with its famous rockbound coast—lobstermen, tourism, and all—serving as the front door for a forest fiefdom.

*H*enry David Thoreau once made the ironic comment that he had "traveled extensively" in his hometown of Concord, Massachusetts. Similarly, we suggest it's possible to travel extensively indeed in the vest-pocket, six-state corner of America called New England. We know, because we've been doing it for years.

New England certainly claims an extensive variety of terrain. Not even the seacoast is all of a piece: Rolling Atlantic breakers shape the broad, sandy barrier beaches of Cape Cod, while calmer waters lap the shores of Long Island Sound, and the pounding surf perpetually hammers the coast of Maine. Inland, the low country of exurban New England, won from the forest by colonial axes, still remains a patchwork of rolling meadows. As you head west and north the hills grow higher, becoming true mountains along Vermont's green cordillera, in the fastnesses of northern New Hampshire where Mount Washington reigns amid its own often frightening weather, and on the lonely massif of Katahdin in Maine, surrounded by a silent ocean of pine.

Of course it would be easy to dart across all these landscapes, north to south or east to west, in less time than it takes to get from one reasonably sized town to another in the vaster regions of the United States. But our own travels have taught us that no other place in America serves up nearly as many reasons to duck off the main road and look for the places large and small that define the local character.

New England is a landscape heavily strewn with the life-size artifacts of tradition and experiment, of raw enterprise and the culture it affords. These places are what this book is about: seaports, craft workshops, battlefields, farms, birthplaces of Presidents and poets, rackety looms, doughty old locomotives, and a great deal more.

It is an old place, New England is, and its legacy is densely textured and splendidly varied. You'd better start driving.

KAY AND BILL SCHELLER

About the Guides

Whale watching off the Massachusetts coast

*N*ATIONAL GEOGRAPHIC'S DRIVING GUIDES TO AMERICA invite you on memorable road trips through the United States and Canada. Intended both as travel planners and companions, each volume guides you on preplanned tours over a wide variety of terrain to the best places to see and things to do. The authors, expert regional travel writers, star-rate (from none to two ★★) the drives and points of interest to make sure you don't miss their favorites.

All distances and drive times are approximate (if you linger, as you should, plan on considerably more time). Recommended seasons are the best times to go, but roads and sites are open all year unless otherwise noted. Besides the stated days of operation, many sites close on national holidays. For the most up-to-date site information, it's best to call ahead when possible.

Then, with this book and a road map, set off on your adventure through this awesomely beautiful land.

MAP KEY and ABBREVIATIONS

National Historical Park	N.H.P.	Featured Drive
National Park		
National Seashore		Interstate Highway 94
National Forest		
State Forest	S.F.	U.S. Federal Highway 12
Forest (Private)		
National Wildlife Refuge	N.W.R.	State Road 29
State Park	S.P.	
State Reservation		County, Local, or Provincial Road A
Reservation	Res.	
Park (Local)		

ADDITIONAL ABBREVIATIONS

E. Br.	*East Branch*
FT.	*Fort*
H.S.	*Historic Site*
HWY.	*Highway*
INTL.	*International*
INTL. H.S.	*International Historic Site*
MEM.	*Memorial*
Mt.-s.	*Mount, Mountain-s*
N.H.S.	*National Historic Site*
REC. AREA	*Recreation Area*
R.R.	*Railroad*
S.B.	*State Beach*
S.H.S.	*State Historic Site*
TRANS.	*Transportation*
W. Br.	*West Branch*
UNIV.	*University*

- - - - - Trail

⊦⊦⊦⊦⊦⊦ Railroad

State or National Border

· · · · · Ferry

⌐⌐⌐⌐⌐ Canal

■ Point of Interest

⊛ State Capital

❙ Dam

= Falls

) (Pass

POPULATION

● **Boston**	500,000 and over
● **Cambridge**	50,000 to under 500,000
● Gurleyville	under 50,000

North Woods

300 miles ● 3 to 4 days ● Early summer through mid-September ● Many bumpy dirt roads. User fee for private logging road.

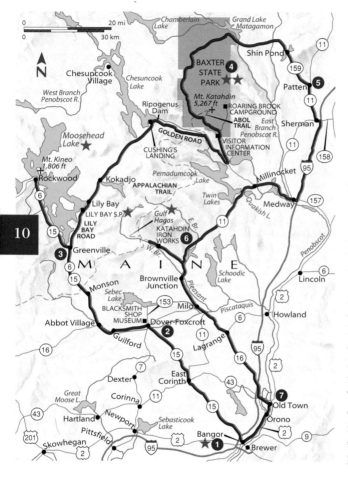

Across Maine's northern counties lies the Maine of legend—the inland empire of silent spruce and fir forests, the domain of the moose and the loon. Here, gargantuan lumber company holdings comprise a virtual state within a state, while New England's largest state park surrounds the lonely massif of Mount Katahdin.

The route begins in Bangor, terminus of the old-time logging drives, then circles north past Maine's largest lake to Baxter State Park. Turning south, the drive links an old ironworks, a spectac-ular chasm, and a lively university town.

With 33,000 resi-dents the biggest city in the Penobscot River Valley, **❶ Bangor ★** feels more like a large town. During the mid-19th century its mills processed some 200 million board feet of lumber annually, and timber barons built mansions that still distinguish the city. Stop by the Chamber of Com-merce *(519 Main St. 207-947-0307)*, next to the 31-foot-high, 1.5-ton **Paul Bunyan Statue,** to pick up a walking tour brochure. Among the must-see stops: The **Isaac Farrar Mansion** *(166 Union St. 207-941-2808. July-Sept. Thurs. or by appt.)*, in the **High Street Historic District,** was designed by Richard Upjohn (1802-1878). He also designed the

Greek Revival **Thomas A. Hill House** *(159 Union St. 207-942-5766. April-Dec. Tues.-Fri., weekends by appt.; donations)*, headquarters of the Bangor Historical Society. Writer Stephen King has made his Italianate villa, the **William Arnold House** *(47 W. Broadway. Private)*, even more distinguished: It stands behind a wrought-iron fence decorated with bats, spiders, and intricate webs.

The **Cole Land Transportation Museum** ★ *(405 Perry Rd. 207-990-3600. May–Veterans Day; adm. fee)* exhibits more than 200 vehicles—everything from antique baby carriages to horse-drawn logging sleds.

Head north out of town on Maine 15 to ❷ **Dover-Foxcroft.** From the town center, pick up Maine 153 north to the **Blacksmith Shop Museum** *(Dawes Rd. 207-564-8618. Mem. Day–Oct.)*, whose 1863 old smithy shop displays original equipment.

Watch for moose in the boggy areas alongside Maine 15 as you wend your way to the tiny town of ❸ **Greenville.** Perched on the south-

Sunrise at Moosehead Lake

ern end of 35-mile-long **Moosehead Lake** ★, which claims over 200 miles of shoreline, the town is the jumping-off point for really getting into the woods.

Tour the lake aboard the ***Katahdin*** ★ ★ *(Waterfront. 207-695-2716. July-Aug. Tues.-Sun., weekends only Mem. Day–June and Sept.; fare)*, a magnificently restored former steamboat (now diesel) that once carried timber booms. You can see steamboat memorabilia both on board and at a small museum back at the landing.

Folsom's Air Service *(207-695-2821)* offers flights from Greenville north to the historic lumbering town of **Chesuncook Village,** where the **Chesuncook Lake House** *(207-745-5330. House, with meals, open late spring–foliage season. Cabins open year-round. Guides, boats, and cross-country ski tours available)* provides the ultimate getaway with its rustic guest rooms and housekeeping cabins. The village is also accessible by boat from Cushing's Landing.

11

Majesty of the Loon

Loons embody the untamed spirit of the wilderness they inhabit, the deep North Woods. Here they move like phantoms on the cold glassy lakes they call home, with their spectral ululations and astonishing ability to dive and resurface far away.

Old Town Canoe Factory Outlet

Northwest of Greenville, several water taxis *(Old Mill Campground 207-534-7333)* leave from **Rockwood** for **Mount Kineo,** a sheer 800-foot cliff that rises out of Moosehead Lake. The summit is accessible via two hiking trails; ask your boat captain to point out the trailheads. To appreciate the cliff's grandeur—and possibly catch sight of nesting peregrine falcons in spring and early summer—have the captain bring you around to the north side. You can find food, lodging, and wonderful views at the **Kineo House** *(207-534-8812. Closed April)*.

Before leaving Greenville, fill the gas tank; there are no services for the next 100 miles. At **Lily Bay State Park★** *(207-695-2700. Staffed May–mid-Oct.; adm. fee)*, sunrise is spectacular from the sandy beach.

The pavement ends and the dirt road begins at **Kokadjo,** whose population is locally described as "five full-time residents." As you head farther north, be wary of the lumber trucks that seem to rule the North Woods. At Great Northern Paper's West Branch Region checkpoint *(staffed May-Nov.; toll)*, pick up information on traveling through the next 40 miles of private woodlands.

After exiting the property, take a sharp left to ❹ **Baxter State Park ★ ★** *(207-723-5140. Camping mid-May–mid-Oct. Advance reservations recommended for campsites. Dogs not permitted. Visitors must register year-round. Adm. fee)*. A magnificent 202,064-acre tract of wilderness whose crowning glory is mile-high **Mount Katahdin,** Baxter is best seen by hiking trail. Before entering the gate, pick up a trail map at the Visitor Information Center. You may wish to stretch your legs on the popular 3.3-mile round-trip hike between **Roaring Brook Campground** and **Basin Ponds.** In summer, plan to arrive by 6 a.m.; park rangers often close the road when the parking lot fills. The 7.6-mile **Abol Trail** is extremely steep and difficult, but it's the shortest route to Baxter Peak at Katahdin's summit, the northern terminus of the Appalachian Trail.

Leaving Baxter, go east to **5** **Patten.** Nine authentic buildings at the **Lumberman's Museum** *(Me. 159. 207-528-2650. Mem. Day–Labor Day Tues.-Sun.; adm. fee)* re-create every aspect of a woodsman's life during the 1800s and early 1900s. Look at the tools, get a sense of the routine—and understand why the cook earned the most pay.

From Millinocket, take Maine 11 south to the turnoff for **6** **Katahdin Iron Works** *(207-965-8135. Checkpoint staffed May-Oct.)*, the remains of an 1840 ironworks and the town that catered to its workers. One of the original 16 charcoal kilns and a blast furnace have been restored.

Katahdin Iron Works

To hike into **Gulf Hagas**★ *(207-965-8135. Adm. fee)*, grandiloquently nicknamed the Grand Canyon of Maine, continue past the ironworks to a North Maine Woods checkpoint. The 6-mile, round-trip hike into the gulf is very steep, but rewarded by fine views of the West Branch Pleasant River. The trail leads to where the river funnels through a 3.5-mile-long, steep-walled gorge and drops almost 400 feet in elevation in a series of magnificent waterfalls. From the main trail it's a short, easy hike to lovely Screw Auger Falls and the Hermitage, a majestic stand of towering white pines.

13

The drive zips south on Maine 11 to Milo, then veers southeast on Maine 16 and Maine 43 to **7** **Old Town.** Having produced canoes for nearly a century, the town is well known in the trade. If you're in the market, stop by the **Old Town Canoe Factory Outlet** *(130 Main St. 207-827-5513. Closed Sun. Oct.-Feb. and Sat. Dec.-Feb.)*, which discounts canoes with visible blemishes.

Hikers in Baxter State Park

US 2 leads south to **Orono,** where the **University of Maine** has several fine museums. The **Hudson Museum**★ *(Maine Center for the Arts Bldg. 207-581-1901. Tues.-Sun.)* explores Native American cultural history in Maine and the United States. A post-and-beam barn holds the **Page Farm and Home Museum** *(207-581-4100. Closed Sun.-Mon. mid-Sept.–mid-May)*, filled with displays on Maine farm life between 1865 and 1940. Prints by Pablo Picasso are among the 5,500-work collection of the **University of Maine Museum of Art**★ *(109 Carnegie Hall. 207-581-3255. Mon.-Fri.)*.

Down East ★

500 miles ● 3 to 4 days ● Late spring through early fall ● Arrive at Acadia National Park early or late in the day (or off-season) to avoid crowds. Park Loop Road closed in winter.

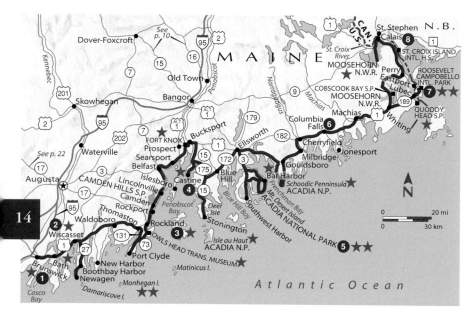

Down East

Why "Down East," a nautical term dating back to the 1800s? Maine's coastline goes both east and north. Since prevailing winds blow from the southwest, schooners heading northeast to Maine from Boston had the wind at their backs—they sailed down wind. Thus the term Down East. Today it refers to the coastal region northeast of Portland.

Meandering north along Maine's fantastically intricate coastline, US 1 explores a ragged landscape of narrow peninsulas and rocky bays, sea-sprayed islands and lonely promontories. Side routes wander off to secluded beaches, tiny lobstering villages, and ferries that transport visitors to remote, windy islands lost in time.

The drive begins in Brunswick, near the head of Casco Bay, and links the old seafaring towns of Wiscasset, Rockland, and Camden on its way to Bar Harbor and hugely popular Acadia National Park. Beyond Bar Harbor the traffic thins as US 1 ambles toward Eastport, Franklin D. Roosevelt's beloved Campobello Island, and Calais, on the Canadian border.

English traders and fishermen settled ❶ **Brunswick**★ (*Chamber of Commerce 207-725-8797*) in the early 1600s. By the mid-1700s it was on its way to becoming the major industrial city in the eastern Casco Bay region. Since 1888 the **Pejepscot Historical Society** (*159 Park Row. 207-729-6606*), named for the Indians who once lived in the area, has worked to preserve the region's history, and maintains three distinct properties. The **Pejepscot Museum** *(Weekdays year-round and Sat. p.m. in summer)* displays changing exhibits in an 1858 Italianate double mansion. Next door stands the 17-room **Skolfield-Whittier House**★ *(Summer–early fall Tues.-Sat.; adm. fee),* a somewhat eerie Victorian time capsule, complete with resident ghosts. The **Joshua L. Chamberlain Museum** *(226 Maine St. Summer–early fall Tues.-Sat.; adm. fee),* home of the Gettysburg hero and former president of Bowdoin College, is a restored hodgepodge billed as a "work in progress." It contains many of Chamberlain's Civil War mementos.

Across the street you'll find the Gothic Revival **First Parish Church** *(Church office, 9 Cleveland St. 207-729-7331),* where Harriet Beecher Stowe is said to have been inspired to write *Uncle Tom's Cabin,* and the 110-acre **Bowdoin College** *(207-725-3000)* campus. Bowdoin's **Peary-MacMillan Arctic Museum**★ *(Hubbard Hall. 207-725-3416. Tues.-Sun.),* named for polar pioneers and Bowdoin alumni Robert Peary and Donald MacMillan, describes their Arctic journeys with artifacts, papers, and natural history specimens.

15

Boothbay Harbor at dusk

Farther east in the shipbuilding center of **Bath**★ *(Chamber of Commerce 207-443-9751),* the **Maine Maritime Museum**★★ *(243 Washington St. 207-443-1316. Adm. fee)* focuses on Maine's seafaring history. Multimedia and hands-on exhibits provide background. You can explore a fishing schooner (when it's in port) and take a boat ride down the Kennebec River past the thriving Bath Iron Works. Before leaving town, drive through the north end, where wealthy shipbuilders built their mansions.

Whether or not ❷ **Wiscasset**★ lives up to its claim—"the prettiest village in Maine"—it's certainly a contender. Wealthy shipping and lumber barons built elaborate mansions and grand public buildings here, and several offer tours. The **Nickels-Sortwell House**★ *(Main and Federal Sts. 207-882-6218. June–mid-Oct. Wed.-Sun.; adm. fee),* built by a sea captain, was later refurbished in the colonial revival style. Overlooking the harbor, the 1807 **Lee-Tucker House** *(Lee and High Sts. 207-882-7364. July-Aug. Tues.-Sun.; adm. fee)* is also known as Castle Tucker.

The plans for the fortlike **Old Jail and Museum** *(Federal St. 207-882-6817. July-Aug. Tues.-Sun.; adm. fee)* were drawn according to the British penal belief that housing criminals in small cells was more humane than keeping them in a large space. On a cheerier note, the **Musical Wonder House** *(18 High St. 207-882-7163 or 800-336-3725. Mid-May–mid-Oct.; adm. fee),* a museum of mechanical instruments, includes music boxes, crank organs, and mechanized birds.

Farther ahead, turn south on Maine 27 to **Boothbay Harbor** *(Chamber of Commerce 207-633-2353).* A popular resort area since the late 1800s, its often crowded harbor area offers all the requisite tourist amenities. Pick up a boat charter to **Damariscove**—the site of one of Maine's earliest permanent European settlements (early 1600s)—or to another nearby island. For a genuine Down East clambake, hop aboard the ***Argo*** *(Pier 6, Fisherman's Wharf. 207-633-7200. Mid-June–Labor Day; fare)* to **Cabbage Island.** Landlubbers can find wonderful coastal views by following Maine 238 to Newagen at the tip of Southport Island.

Sampling the stocks at Boothbay Railway Village

US 1 winds farther east to **Waldoboro** *(Chamber of Commerce 207-832-4883),* where exhibits in the **Waldoborough Historical Society Museum** *(Upper Main St. Daily mid-June–Labor Day, weekends until early Oct.)* chronicle the town's 19th-century commercial heritage. Earlier history is summed up in the **Old German Church cemetery** *(Bremen Road)* on a tombstone: "This town was settled in 1748 by Germans who immigrated to this Place with the promise and expectation of finding a prosperous city, instead of which they found nothing but wilderness."

Once a busy shipbuilding town, **Thomaston** *(Chamber of Commerce 207-596-0376)* now bustles with another trade: The **Maine State Prison Showroom** *(Main St. 207-354-2535 ext. 272)* sells wood products made by inmates. It's worth a visit. On a hill above town, **Montpelier** *(207-354-8062. Late May–mid-Oct. Tues.-Sun.; adm. fee)* is a reconstruction of the federal house once belonging to Maj. Gen.

16

Henry Knox (1750-1806), the first U.S. secretary of war.

Down Maine 131 in **Port Clyde,** the **Monhegan Boat Line** *(207-372-8848. Call for schedule; reservations required. Fare)* takes visitors to **Monhegan Island★★,** a fishing community and artists retreat 11 miles out at sea.

Farther east on Maine 73, anything goes at the **Owls Head Transportation Museum★** *(207-594-4418.*

Pemaquid Point Lighthouse, New Harbor

Adm. fee), a collection of antique yet still working modes of transport—carriages, bicycles, autos, airplanes. During summer events you might take a ride in a Model T Ford or watch World War II fighters roar by in an air show.

The busy harbor town of **❸ Rockland★** *(Chamber of Commerce 207-596-0376)*, known for its bountiful lobster harvest, also claims the state's largest windjammer fleet. Several schooners offer cruises from the harbor. The **Rockland Harbor Trail** follows the historic working waterfront.

The **Farnsworth Art Museum★★** *(352 Main St. 207-596-6457. Adm. fee)* features a fine collection of American art, including works by Maine artists. Among the standouts: George Bellows' "Sea and Fog of Monhegan Island" and Andrew Wyeth's "Her Room." Admission to the circa 1850 Greek Revival **Farnsworth Homestead** *(Mem. Day–mid-Oct.)* next door is included in the entrance fee. Stop by the **Shore Village Museum** *(Grand Army Hall, 104 Limerock St. 207-594-0311. June–mid-Oct.; donations)* for a look at its eclectic collection of Civil War memorabilia, carved tusks, ship models, and many lighthouse artifacts.

Just up US 1 is picturesque **Camden** *(Chamber of Commerce 207-236-4404 or 800-223-5459)*, a shipbuilding town dating from the late 18th century. In the early 1900s it, along with tiny nearby Rockport, began attracting wealthy summer residents, mainly from Boston and Philadelphia. Enjoy the shops, restaurants, and galleries, and stroll down to the harbor, where windjammers offer cruises along the coast.

Just north of town, the 5,527-acre **Camden Hills State Park** *(207-236-3109. Staffed May–mid-Oct.; adm. fee)* invites you to hike, camp, and picnic. Take the short road up

Farnsworth Art Museum, Rockland

780-foot **Mount Battie** for fine views of Penobscot Bay.

At Lincolnville Beach hop the state ferry *(207-734-6935. Fare)* for a 20-minute ride to **Islesboro,** where you'll find good beaches and an entertaining display of local history at the **Isleboro Sailors' Memorial Museum** *(Mem. Day–Labor Day Mon.-Sat.; donations),* next to the 1850 Grindle Point Lighthouse. It's possible to arrange a ride from the island to 70-acre **Warren Island State Park** *(207-596-2253. Mid-May–mid-Oct.; fare),* where you can hike and picnic.

From the late 1700s to the late 1800s, **Searsport** *(Chamber of Commerce 207-548-6510)* shipyards built some 250 sailing vessels. Eight historic buildings at the **Penobscot Marine Museum** ★ *(Church St. at US 1. 207-548-2529. Mem. Day–mid-Oct.; adm. fee)* exhibit artifacts, paintings, ship models, and films. See the photos of early ship captains in the Old Town Hall, and don't miss the scrimshaw exhibit.

In Prospect, **Fort Knox** ★ *(Fort Knox State Park. 207-469-7719. Fort open May-Oct.; adm. fee)* is Maine's largest granite fortification, built to protect the Penobscot River Valley from the British in response to a boundary dispute with New Brunswick. Construction began in 1844, but the elaborate plans were never completed.

Make sure you have a good road map before plunging into the rat's nest of roads in the Castine and Blue Hill areas, which occupy a jagged peninsula between Penobscot and Blue Hill Bays. More than 100 plaques around town document the 200-year struggle by four countries to possess strategic ❹ **Castine** ★. Pick up a walking tour brochure at the Town Office *(Emerson Hall, Court St. 207-326-4502).* In addition to exhibits of prehistoric and Native American artifacts, the **Wilson Museum** *(Perkins St. 207-326-8753. Mem. Day–Sept. Tues.-Sun.)* encompasses the circa 1765 **John Perkins House** *(July-Aug. Wed. and Sun. p.m.; adm. fee),* Castine's oldest surviving building.

On the way south to Deer Isle and Stonington, stop at **Caterpillar Hill Rest Area** for panoramic views of Penobscot Bay. Then follow Maine 15 over Deer Isle Bridge to the lobstering village of **Stonington,** whose once thriving granite quarrying industry is reviving. The **Isle-Au-Haut Company** *(Atlantic Ave. Hardware Dock. 207-367-5193 days, 367-2355 eves. Mid-June–early Sept.; fare)* ferries passengers to

Isle au Haut★, which includes part of Acadia National Park.

Backtrack on Maine 15 and head north to **Blue Hill.** This one-time shipbuilding town is now a hub for artists and craftspeople. You'll find wheel-thrown pottery made from locally dug clay at **Rackcliffe Pottery** *(Me. 172. 207-374-2297. Closed Sun. Sept.-June)* and **Rowantree's Pottery** *(Me. 177. 207-374-5535. Closed Sun. Sept. June).*

The route goes north to US 1 at Ellsworth, then south to **Mount Desert Island,** home of ❺ **Acadia National Park★★** *(207-288-3338. Most of Park Loop Rd. closed in winter; adm. fee).* The glacier-carved island is a phenomenal geological grab bag of mountains, lakes, cliffs, forests, beaches, rugged shoreline, and the only true fjord—**Somes Sound★** —on the U.S. Atlantic coast. (Some geologists consider the lower Hudson River another.) As you enter the park, stop at the **Hulls Cove Visitor Center** *(May-Oct.)* to get your bearings. The 27-mile **Park Loop Road** takes in some of the park's most popular sites, including **Sand Beach★**, **Thunder Hole★**, and **Otter Cliffs.** The **Jordan Pond House** *(207-276-3316. Mid-May–late Oct.)* serves lunch, tea, and dinner overlooking a bucolic pond. Hike or drive Cadillac Mountain Road to the summit of 1,530-foot **Cadillac Mountain★**, the highest point on the Atlantic coast north of Brazil and, from October to early May, the first place on the continental U.S. to see sunrise. At the **Abbe Museum** *(207-288-3519. Mid-May–late Oct.; adm. fee),* exhibits, hands-on activities, and craft workshops focus on Maine's Native American heritage.

In **Bar Harbor★** *(Chamber of Commerce 207-288-3393),* the town's legendary popularity as a turn-of-the-century summer playground for the rich is evident in the large number of mansions, or "cottages." The fine stained-glass window collection at **St. Saviour's Church★** *(Mt. Desert St. 207-288-4215. Tours in July-Aug.)* includes several from the late 1800s by Louis Comfort Tiffany. A shore path begins at the Town Municipal Pier and follows **Frenchman Bay** to upper Main Street.

Setting sail from Camden

Leaving town, take Maine 233 (Eagle Lake Road) west to Maine 3 and Maine 198, looping around **Somes Sound.**

Lobster Tales

When a lobster is hatched, it's about the size of a flea. As it matures, it successively moults its rigid exoskeleton, or shell, and grows until its new shell hardens. A lobster moults perhaps ten times in its first year, during which it will grow to be only two inches long. It takes five to eight years to weigh a pound, which is about as small a lobster as you'll ever see on a dinner plate— although legal limits are based on length, not weight. Older lobsters shed their shells only once a year; a really big lobster—ten pounds or more—may have been dodging traps and predators for as many as 20 years.

View of Bar Harbor and Frenchman Bay from Cadillac Mountain, Mount Desert Island

At Maine 102, turn south to the fishing town of **Southwest Harbor** *(Chamber of Commerce 207-244-9264 or 800-423-9264)*. A hand-carved, life-size bald eagle greets visitors to the **Wendell Gilley Museum of Bird Carving**★ *(Herrick Rd. 207-244-7555. June-Oct. Tues.-Sun.; May, Nov., Dec. Fri.-Sun.; adm. fee)*, which displays many of the 6,000 birds Gilley carved before his death in 1983.

Rejoining US 1, the route rambles ever east. At Maine 186, detour south to the **Schoodic Peninsula**★ and another parcel of Acadia National Park. The park's 7.2-mile shore drive here, while not as dramatic as the Park Loop Road, is far less crowded and very scenic.

Built in 1818 for a rich lumber dealer, the **Ruggles House** *(.25 mile off US 1. 207-483-4637. June–mid-Oct.; adm. fee)* in ❻ **Columbia Falls** displays many original furnishings. The flying staircase is a work of art, as is the intricate woodwork supposedly carved with a penknife by a British craftsman.

In **Machias,** the gambrel-roofed 1770 **Burnham Tavern** *(Me. 192. 207-255-4432. Mid-June–Sept. Mon.-Fri.; adm. fee)* claims a significant spot in Revolutionary War history. In 1775 colonists met here to plan the capture of the British man-of-war *Margaretta*. They seized the ship in one of the

Revolution's first naval battles, but in retaliation the British burned the town of Falmouth.

At Whiting, veer east to **Lubec** *(Chamber of Commerce 207-733-4522)*, the easternmost town in the United States. The candy cane-striped **West Quoddy Head Light★,** now closed, at **Quoddy Head State Park★** *(207-733-0911. Mid-May–mid-Oct.; adm. fee)* stands on the nation's easternmost point of land. From there you can enjoy magnificent ocean views and some marvelous hiking trails, including one through a peat bog. The park's steep ledges offer an excellent vantage point for the famous **Bay of Fundy** tides, which rise as high as 30 feet.

Just over the Franklin D. Roosevelt Memorial Bridge on **Campobello Island,** in New Brunswick, Canada, is the ❼ **Roosevelt Campobello International Park★★** *(506-752-2922. Mem. Day–Columbus Day; grounds open year-round. New Brunswick time one hour later than Maine time).* Franklin D. Roosevelt spent most of his boyhood summers here, and his life and times feel as if they've been flash-frozen in the 34-room "cottage" the family occupied from 1909 to 1921. The 2,800-acre memorial park features formal gardens and wooded paths to the sea.

Farther east, US 1 passes through the **Edmunds Unit** of the 24,446-acre **Moosehorn National Wildlife Refuge** *(207-454-7161)* and **Cobscook Bay State Park** *(207-726-4412. Mid-May–Labor Day).*

The drive soon offers fine views of the **St. Croix River**'s red cliffs. In the middle of the river, on **Saint Croix Island** *(No ferry service),* French explorers Samuel de Champlain and Sieur de Monts established in 1604 North America's first documented European settlement

Roosevelt Cottage, Campobello Island

north of St. Augustine, Florida. The **Saint Croix Island International Historic Site** *(Off US 1. For info call Acadia National Park at 207-288-3338),* 8 miles south of Calais, commemorates the settlement.

Passing through ❽ **Calais,** one of the busiest ports of entry along the U.S.-Canada border, the drive ends at the **Baring Unit★** *(Charlotte Rd. 207-454-3521)* of Moosehorn National Wildlife Refuge. In spring and summer, look for nesting bald eagles along Charlotte Road.

From here, if you'd rather not retrace your steps, return to Bangor on Maine 9, then back to Brunswick via I-95.

**370 miles ● 3 to 4 days ● Late spring through early fall
● After late October, be prepared for snow in the north.**

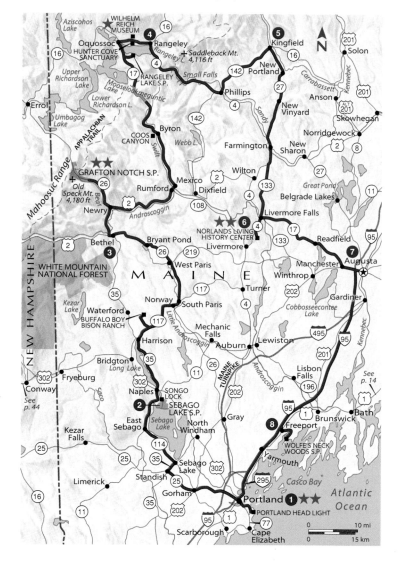

Think of Maine, and the images that come to mind are the famous rockbound coast and the North Woods's vast ocean of pines. This ramble takes in a lesser known Maine, or rather several Maines: the cosmopolitan charm of Portland, the rolling hills of the western lakes district, and the attractions of two capitals—one of state government and the other of discount shopping.

Beginning in Portland, the drive winds north to link Sebago, Long, and Rangeley Lakes. After skirting the southern fringes of the great Maine woods, it dips south to the capital of Augusta and rejoins the seacoast at Freeport.

Almost one-fourth of Maine's population resides in ❶ **Portland**★★ *(Visitor Information Center, 305 Commercial St. 207-772-5800).* Completely rebuilt after a fire in 1866, the city has preserved most of its Victorian-era architecture and flavor. The Visitor Center has a walking tour brochure of the city's four major areas: the Old Port Exchange, the Downtown Arts District, the Eastern Promenade, and the Western Promenade. With its cobblestone streets and gas lamps, the six-block redbrick-and-granite **Old Port** best captures the feel of early seaport days. Here you can catch a cruise around the **Calendar Islands,** a whale-watching excursion, or a fishing charter.

23

Portland's Old Port Exchange area

The Italianate **Victoria Mansion**★ *(109 Danforth St. 207-772-4841. May-Oct. Tues.-Sun.; adm. fee),* built between 1858 and 1860, retains the ornate interior and elaborate furnishings typical of its era. The 1785 **Wadsworth-Longfellow House**★ *(485-489 Congress St. 207-879-0427. June-Oct. Tues.-Sun.; adm. fee),* Portland's first all-brick dwelling, was the childhood home of Henry Wadsworth Longfellow. You'll see family furnishings and mementos. The **Portland Museum of Art**★ *(7 Congress Sq. 207-775-6148. Closed Mon. early Oct.–early July; adm. fee),* the state's largest art museum, houses a comprehensive collection of 18th- and 19th-century European and American art, with an emphasis on local artists such as summer resident Winslow Homer. Next door, hands-on science and art exhibits pack the **Children's Museum of Maine** *(142 Free St. 207-828-1234. Closed Mon.-Tues. during school year; adm. fee).*

From Portland, head south toward Cape Elizabeth and follow signs to **Portland Head Light** *(Fort Williams Park. 207-799-2661. Museum open daily June-Oct., weekends only April-May and Nov.-Dec.; adm. fee),* the state's oldest lighthouse (1791). The museum, in the former keeper's quarters, chronicles the history of the light and fort, built in 1898.

Return to Portland and take Maine 25 west to **Standish** and the 1789 **Marrett House** *(617-227-3956. Mid-June–Sept. Tues., Thurs., and Sat.-Sun. p.m.; adm. fee).* For more than 150 years, each generation has altered the architecture and furnishings, creating a visual document of changing tastes.

Moose in the Rangeley Lakes region

Travel along the shoreline of Sebago Lake to ❷ **Sebago Lake State Park** (207-287-3821. *Adm. fee*), a popular 1,342-acre spot for swimming and fishing. Down the entrance road you'll see **Songo Lock,** the last in a series of 28 hand-operated locks that were constructed in 1829 along a canal and linked Songo Lake and Portland.

On Long Lake, the resort town of **Naples** (*Information Center 207-693-3285*) offers everything from Jet-ski rentals to seaplane rides. The ***Songo River Queen II*** (*207-693-6861. Daily July–Labor Day, June and Sept. weekends only; adm. fee*), an old-fashioned riverboat, gives lake tours and passes through Songo Lock.

For terrific lake and mountain views—and bison—continue north on Maine 35, then east on Maine 117 toward Norway. The bison, at least eight of them, *do* roam at the **Buffalo Boy Bison Ranch** (*440 Baker Hill Rd. 207-583-2761 or 800-78-BISON. Year-round; barbecues June-Sept. Sat.-Sun.*), run by a former New York chef who has combined homesteading with a love of cooking. The result? Bison burger barbecues, a bakery serving gourmet foods—and roaming bison.

Follow Maine 117 through Norway to South Paris, then take Maine 26 north. **Perham's of West Paris** (*Junction of Me. 26 and Me. 219. 207-674-2341 or 800-371-GEMS*) awaits in the middle of Oxford County, where gemstones have been mined since the 1800s. A small museum displays Maine minerals and gems. Try your luck at rock hounding at one of four quarries within 10 miles of the shop, and keep whatever treasures you find.

At **Bryant Pond,** take a moment to look in the window of the tiny **Bryant Pond Telephone Museum** (*Rumford Ave. 207-336-9911. By appt.*). The local telephone company was the last in the country to stop using hand-cranked magneto phones; the giant switchboard inside was in service until 1983.

Farming, once the major industry in the Androscoggin River community of ❸ **Bethel** (*Chamber of Commerce, 30 Cross St. 207-824-2282*), has been displaced by the manufacture of wood products. A walking tour booklet of the historic district, available at the chamber, includes a visit to the 1813 **Dr. Moses Mason House** *(14 Broad St. 207-824-2908. Mem. Day–Labor Day or by appt.; adm. fee),* a nine-room, period-furnished residence known for its magnificent wall murals.

Head north from Bethel on Maine 26 and US 2 to the turnoff for **Grafton Notch State Park★★** *(207-824-2912. Mid-May–mid-Oct.).* The most magnificent of the geological phenomena along this mountainous route is also the most accessible at **Screw Auger Falls.** Just off the road, the cascading waters of the Bear River have worn giant potholes in the bedrock. Farther ahead you'll find **Mother Walker Falls,** a long, narrow gorge; **Moose Cave Gorge,** boasting a .25-mile loop trail; and **Table Rock,** hovering above Maine's most extensive slab cave system.

From Newry, US 2 weaves through a rolling landscape of pine forests, one of the prettiest parts of the state. At the paper mill town of Rumford, head north on Maine 17 toward Oquossoc and the **Rangeley Lakes region.** The route joins the Swift River, which over millions of years carved **Coos Canyon** into the bedrock near Byron. The nation's first gold strike is said to have taken place in Byron, in 1848. The folks at the **Coos Canyon**

Beaver Mountain Pond, off Maine 17

Wilderness Campground *(Me. 17. 207-364-3880. Mid-April–Nov.)* will give you some pointers and rent equipment if you want to try gold panning yourself.

For the next 20 miles, the drive twists and turns up into the mountains, crosses the Appalachian Trail, and provides periodic turnouts overlooking breathtaking vistas.

The 691-acre **Rangeley Lake State Park** *(207-864-3858. Mid-May–Sept.; adm. fee),* on the lake's southern shore, has campgrounds, a swimming beach, and a boat launch. Fishing enthusiasts know all about its big landlocked salmon.

At Oquossoc turn east on Maine 4/16 and take a winding half-mile road to the **Wilhelm Reich Museum ★,** also known as **Orgonon** *(Orgonon–Dodge Pond Rd. 207-864-3443. July-Aug. Tues.-Sun., Sun. only in Sept., nature center open year-round; adm. fee).* The scientist who developed the controversial theory of "orgone," or universal energy, built this native fieldstone laboratory-observatory in 1948. Even skeptics will enjoy the pastoral setting, magnificent views of the lake region, and hiking trails.

If you're quiet—and extremely patient—you may spot deer, moose, bear, and other creatures in the forests and wetlands of the **Hunter Cove Sanctuary** *(Off Me. 4/16. 207-781-2330),* across the road.

Set among the six major lakes that make up the Rangeley Lakes region, the former logging town of ❹ **Rangeley** *(Chamber of Commerce 207-864-5364 or 800-MT-LAKES)* retains its frontier charm despite having served tourists for well over a century. Farther ahead at the **Small Falls Rest Area,** a path wanders across the cataracts where Chandler Mill Stream and Sandy River meet. Nearby, the Appalachian Trail ascends to the top of 4,116-foot **Saddleback Mountain.**

In Phillips, head north on Maine 142 to ❺ **Kingfield,** home of the **Stanley Museum ★** *(School St. 207-265-2729. Tues.-Sun., closed April and Nov.; adm. fee).* The museum honors the talented Stanley family, best known for twins Francis Edgar and Freelan Oscar, who in 1897 invented the Stanley Steamer—a steam-powered automobile. You also learn about other family members, including the automakers' sister, Chansonetta, a superb photographer. Three beautifully preserved Steamers are on display.

Continue south through Farmington to Livermore Falls, and take Maine 4 farther south. The 450-acre ❻ **Norlands Living History Center ★ ★** *(Norlands Rd., off Me. 4. 207-897-4366. July-Aug., weekends through Columbus Day; adm. fee)* invites visitors to observe—and even participate in—a genuine, late 19th-century farming experience. Among buildings open for tours at the working farm: a one-room schoolhouse, farmer's cottage, church, and Victorian homestead. In the house, late 19th-century ceiling decorations

First Earmuffs

Fifteen-year-old Chester Greenwood of Farmington, Maine, was out ice skating one day in the winter of 1873. When his ears could no longer stand the cold, he went indoors and set to work. The lad took a length of wire and attached fur and cloth to either end, then installed the new apparatus under his hat. Four years later he patented his invention—and marketed it as Chester Greenwood's Champion Ear Protectors. The resourceful adolescent had given the world earmuffs.

26

have been restored by a local artist.

Return to Livermore Falls and drive east on Maine 17 to the state capital of ❼ **Augusta** *(Chamber of Commerce 207-623-4559)*. Settled in the 1600s by Pilgrims who established a trading post on the Kennebec River, the city is now central Maine's economic hub. A classical statue of a woman holding a pine torch—representative of Maine's state tree—stands atop the 185-foot, copper-domed **State House** *(Capitol Complex. 207-287-2301. Call for tour information)*, designed in 1829 by Charles Bulfinch. On the State House grounds, the **Maine State Museum** ★★ *(207-287-2301)* presents exhibits on the state's natural environment, social history, and manufacturing heritage. The governor resides at **Blaine House** *(192 State St. 207-287-2121. Call in advance)*, an 1833 colonial revival mansion that has been remodeled twice.

Costumed guide at Norlands Living History Center

New England's oldest surviving wooden fort, **Old Fort Western** ★ *(16 Cony St. 207-626-2385. Daily Memorial Day–Labor Day, weekends through Columbus Day; adm. fee)* was built in 1754 on the banks of the Kennebec River. Knowledgeable costumed staff interpret its history as a garrisoned fort and trading center.

27

For a total immersion shopping experience follow I-95 south to ❽ **Freeport** *(Merchants Association 207-865-1212 or 800-865-1994)*. Here in 1912 Leon Leonwood Bean began selling hunting shoes from a tiny store. Today, **L.L. Bean** *(95 Main St. 207-865-4761 or 800-341-4341. Open 24 hours)* is a huge, labyrinthine retail operation claiming some 3.5 million customers a year. The **L.L. Bean Factory Store** *(Depot St.)* has been a magnet for more than 120 other outlet stores, all advertising heavily discounted prices.

Blaine House in Augusta

For a breath of fresh air, head to **Wolfe's Neck Woods State Park** *(106 Wolf Neck Rd. 207-865-4465)*, a peaceful natural area amid the populous mid-coast region, and stroll along the half-mile **Casco Bay Trail,** which overlooks an osprey sanctuary on Googins Island.

Coastal Villages★

**75 miles ● 2 to 3 days ● Spring through fall
● Roads along the coast can be crowded in summer,
especially weekends.**

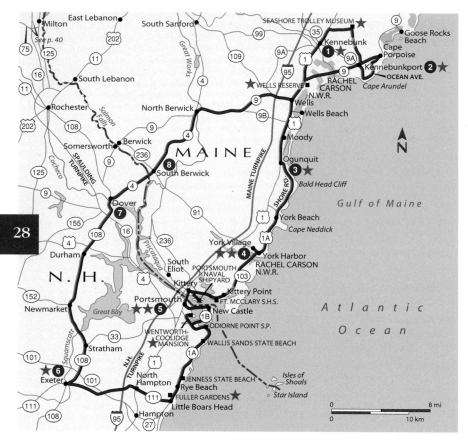

This two-state route combines the southernmost
reaches of Maine's rugged coast with the gardens, colonial mansions, and busy downtown of New Hampshire's
only seaport. At one end is a seaside presidential retreat;
at the other, an ivied prep school town.

Beginning in Kennebunk, Maine, the drive visits the
oceanside towns of Kennebunkport and Ogunquit on the
way to Portsmouth, New Hampshire. After following most
of New Hampshire's abbreviated coastline, it turns inland
to Exeter and Dover, then crosses back over the Maine
border at South Berwick and returns to Kennebunk.

Legacy of the fortunes made from 19th-century
shipbuilding are the lovely mansions and houses that line

the historic district in
❶ Kennebunk★
*(Chamber of Commerce
207-967-0857).* The **Brick
Store Museum** *(117 Main
St. 207-985-4802. Tues.-
Sat.; adm. fee)* offers architectural walking tours of
20 of the houses.

Nubble Light at sunset, York

Drive north out of
town on US 1, and turn
right on Log Cabin Road
to the **Seashore Trolley
Museum★** *(207-967-2712. May-Oct.; adm. fee).* One of the
nation's oldest and largest mass transit museums, it houses
more than 225 antique trolley cars.

The drive continues south on Log Cabin Road to
❷ Kennebunkport★ *(Chamber of Commerce 207-967-
0857).* A shipbuilding center before it became a popular
resort, the resort town is rich in 18th- and 19th-century
architecture. The Kennebunkport Historical Society maintains the 1853 Greek Revival **Nott House** *(8 Maine St. 207-
967-2751. Mid-June–mid-Oct. Wed.-Sat. p.m.; adm. fee),* with
original furnishings and wallpaper. Call about guided walking tours of the historic district. **Dock Square,** in the town
center, has shops, galleries, and restaurants.

Head south from the square for a drive up the coast
along Cape Arundel. On the way, stop at **Indian Whale
Watch** *(207-967-5912. June-Sept.; fare)* at Arundel Wharf to
arrange a whale-watching tour, or at the Nonantum Resort
to line up a lobster boat cruise with **Capt. Dave Bond**
(207-967-2921. June-Aug.; fare). That grand estate overlooking the ocean on the right—the one with the unwelcom-
ing security gate—is **Walkers Point,** summer abode of
former President George Bush.

After rounding the cape, follow Wildes District Road
and Maine 9 east into **Cape Porpoise,** home of the area's
lobster and fishing fleets. From the pier, you can see **Goat
Island Lighthouse,** built in 1834. In summer the fleets'
catch can be sampled at several local restaurants and lobster pounds. **Silica Gallery** *(Pier Rd. 207-967-0133)* exhibits
the work of 53 artists in contemporary hand-blown glass.

Return to Kennebunkport on Maine 9, and continue
farther west to US 1. Turn south and watch on the left for

29

Strawbery Banke

By the 1950s, the Portsmouth neighborhood now preserved as Strawbery Banke Museum was showing its age. Its houses dated as far back as 1695, and the busy commercial wharves that had lined Puddle Dock, as the area was stilll sometimes called, had disappeared with the filling of the inlet that connected them to the harbor. The sharp scythe of urban renewal stood ready to level this crumbling quarter—until a community coalition talked sense to the city fathers, and formed the nonprofit preservation group that administers Strawbery Banke Museum today. The restoration began in 1963 with the circa 1762 Chase House and the 1811 Goodwin Mansion.

Strawbery Banke, Portsmouth

Laudholm Farm Road and the **Wells National Estuarine Research Reserve** ★ *(207-646-1555. Visitor Center closed weekends Nov.-April)*, a 1,600-acre preserve of fields, forests, wetlands, and beach headquartered at the historic Laudholm Farm. The Visitor Center, in a restored 1717 farmhouse, offers exhibits and trail maps.

Farther south in **Wells,** you'll find the **Wells Auto Museum** *(US 1. 207-646-9064. Daily mid-June–Sept., weekends only Mem. Day–mid-June and Oct.–Columbus Day; adm. fee)*. Rooms display 70 gas, steam, and electric cars, including a 1907 Stanley Steamer, a Pierce Arrow, and a Gearless Metz, as well as a collection of operating antique coin games.

Continue south to ❸ **Ogunquit** ★ *(Chamber of Commerce 207-646-2939)*, a picturesque—and crowded—summer resort with 3.5 miles of beach. At one time the town teemed with art galleries, but most have been converted to shops. Among the few that have held on, the **Shore Road Gallery** *(112 Shore Rd. 207-646-5046. Mem. Day–Columbus Day Thurs.-Mon.)* represents nationally known New England artists. From scenic **Perkins Cove,** the 1.25-mile **Marginal Way Walk** ★ ★ follows the shore atop rugged cliffs, offering spectacular views of sea and sky.

From Ogunquit Square, take the Shore Road to the **Ogunquit Museum of American Art** ★ *(207-646-4909. July-Sept.; adm. fee)*. Overlooking the ocean, this beautiful, small museum exhibits an extensive permanent collection of 20th-century American art, including works by Marsden Hartley. A few miles past the museum is the **Cliff House** *(207-361-1000. Closed Jan.-March)*, a resort whose perch atop Bald Head Cliff assures fine ocean vistas with meals.

Continue on the Shore Road to US 1A and the Yorks—past the boardwalk at Short Sands Beach, Cape Neddick and its historic **Nubble Light,** and Long Sands Beach—to historic ❹ **York Village** ★ ★ *(Chamber of Commerce 207-363-4422)*. The **Old York Historical Society** ★ ★ *(140 Lindsay Rd. 207-363-4974. Mid-June–Sept. Tues.-Sun.; adm. fee)* gives tours of seven historic buildings, including the 1719 **Old Gaol,** one of the oldest English colonial public buildings in the country.

The 1718 **Sayward-Wheeler House** *(79 Barrell Ln. Extension. 603-436-3205. June–mid-Oct. Wed.-Sun. p.m.; adm. fee)*, overlooking **York Harbor,** belonged to a prosperous West Indies merchant. The 1-mile **Fisherman's Walk** to York Harbor Beach borders the property.

The drive proceeds south on Maine 103 to **Fort**

McClary State Historic Site *(Kittery Point Rd. 207-439-2845. Mem. Day–Sept.; adm. fee).* The hexagonal blockhouse perched atop **Kittery Point** was built in 1844, adding to fortifications first begun in the early 18th century to hold off the French, pirates, and Indians.

Portsmouth Harbor

Across the state border is the gem of New Hampshire's 18-mile seacoast, ❺ **Portsmouth**★★ *(Chamber of Commerce 603-436-1118).* The compact little city retains the grandeur of its 18th-century maritime heyday without ever seeming fusty or museumlike. Early settlers saw the commercial possibilities of the fertile land at the mouth of the Piscataqua River and built an economy based on the fishing, shipbuilding, and timber industries, which still exist today. **Portsmouth Naval Shipyard** *(207-438-3550. Museum open by appt.),* one of the nation's oldest, occupies Seavey Island between Portsmouth and Kittery, Maine.

Most of Portsmouth's attractions are within walking distance of each other. Begin at **Market Square,** the cultural heart of the city. Here the chamber operates an information kiosk and sells an area guide that includes a walking tour of 30 historic properties on the **Portsmouth Trail**★.

Across from the magnificent formal gardens of **Prescott Park** sprawls the 10-acre **Strawbery Banke Museum**★★ *(Visitor Center on Marcy St. 603-433-1100. Mid-April–early Nov.; adm. fee).* Located within the confines of 17th-century Portsmouth, it preserves 42 houses and commercial buildings from virtually every era of the city's history. Costumed potters, boat builders, and others interpret the different lives lived on these narrow streets, and four period gardens grace the grounds. See sidebar p. 30.

Visit the nearby **St. John's Church** *(101 Chapel St. 603-436-8283)* to look at one of the four Vinegar Bibles in the United States—with the misprint of "vinegar" for "vineyard"—as well as the nation's oldest operating pipe organ

Exeter Academy Quadrangle, Exeter

32

(1708). The **U.S.S. *Albacore*** *(603-436-3680. Closed Tues.-Wed. Labor Day–Mem. Day; adm. fee)*, an experimental submarine built at Portsmouth Naval Shipyard in 1953, now resides across North Mill Pond at Albacore Park. Tours of the 205-by-27-foot sub highlight the cramped but orderly existence of its 55-man crew.

A nine-island archipelago makes up the **Isles of Shoals,** 10 miles out at sea. The islands' colorful history—of pirates, hidden treasure, shipwrecks, and summer hotels—is recounted aboard the Isles of Shoals Steamship Company's excursions *(Barker Wharf. 603-431-5500 or 800-441-4620. May-Oct.; fare)*. Stops include **Star Island,** site of a once-thriving colonial-era fishing village.

Head out of Portsmouth on N.H. 1B to **New Castle,** founded as a fishing village in the late 1600s. In December 1774, four months before Paul Revere's historic ride, some 400 colonists raided **Fort Constitution** *(N.H. 1B. 603-436-1552)* in an action that anticipated the coming Revolutionary War. Interpretive panels narrate the fort's history.

Turn left out of the fort and stay on N.H. 1B to the T-intersection, then turn right onto N.H. 1A to Little Harbor Road. The 1710 **Wentworth Coolidge Mansion★** *(603-436-6607. Daily mid-June–Aug., Mem. Day–mid-June weekends only; adm. fee)* was the 42-room official residence of the state's first royal governor, who served from 1741 to 1767.

From the mansion, backtrack to N.H. 1A and head south to **Odiorne Point,** where Scottish and English fishermen landed in 1623 and created the state's first European settlement. Today, bunkers from the 1940s Fort Dearborn still lie under mounds of earth at **Odiorne Point State Park** *(N.H. 1A, Rye. 603-436-7406. Adm. fee)* and its **Seacoast Science Center** *(Closed Mon. in winter)*. Hiking trails lead to a variety of environments in the park's 330 acres. The center's exhibits explain the area's natural and cultural history.

N.H. 1A winds farther south, past **Wallis Sands State Beach** *(603-436-9404. Adm. fee in season)* and **Jenness State Beach.** Just beyond some imposing summer mansions, look for the sign leading to **Fuller Gardens ★** *(10 Willow Ave. 603-964-5414. Mid-May–mid-Oct.; adm. fee)*. In the early 1920s, noted landscape architect Arthur Shurcliff designed this 2-acre, colonial revival garden.

Continue south on N.H. 1A, then west on N.H. 111 to
❻ Exeter★ *(Chamber of Commerce 603-772-2411).* Rich in
colonial and Revolutionary War history, the handsome
town is the site of **Phillips Exeter Academy,** founded in
1781. The original section of the **Gilman Garrison House**
*(12 Water St. 603-436-3205. June–mid-Oct. Tues., Thurs., Sat.-Sun.
p.m.; adm. fee)* was constructed of massive, square-sawed
logs; a more elegant wing was added in the mid-1700s.
The Ladd-Gilman House and Folsom Tavern hold the
American Independence Museum★ *(1 Governors Lane.
603-772-2622. May-Oct. Wed.-Sun. p.m.; adm. fee),* whose collection tells about Exeter's role in the American Revolution.

❼ Dover, north on N.H. 108, is the state's oldest permanent settlement and the home of one of its most eclectic museums. The **Woodman Institute**★ *(182-190 Central
Ave. 603-742-1038. Tues.-Sat. p.m.)* actually constitutes three
museums. The 1818 **Woodman House** offers a hodgepodge of natural history and war memorabilia, including
Abraham Lincoln's saddle. In 1915, a horse and four men
moved the 1675 **Dame Garrison House** 3 miles to institute grounds, where it's now guarded by a Napoleonic
cannon and a sperm whale jawbone. Historical artifacts
pack the nearby **Hale House,** built in 1818.

33

Take N.H./Maine 4 east to **❽ South Berwick,** Maine,
the longtime residence of Sarah Orne Jewett, whose nov-
els and stories capture the region's late 19th-century flavor. Jewett spent most of her life in her
grandfather's Georgian home, now the **Sarah
Orne Jewett House** *(5 Portland St. 603-436-3205.
June–mid-Oct. Tues., Thurs., and Sat.-Sun. p.m.;
adm. fee),* begun in 1774 and completed after
the Revolutionary War. When built, it was considered the most elegant house in town, and
the hand-carved woodwork and mica-flecked
wallpaper—designed to reflect candlelight—are
no less lovely today.

Northern New England's autumn color

Merchant Jonathan Hamilton built his Georgian
Hamilton House★ *(Vaughan's Ln. 603-436-3205. June–mid-
Oct. Tues., Thurs., Sat.-Sun. p.m.; adm. fee)* about 1785. Boston
friends of Miss Jewett bought it in 1899, restored it, deco-
rated the walls with murals, and furnished it with antiques.
Don't miss the cottage just beyond the Italianate garden.

From South Berwick, the drive returns to Kennebunk
via Maine 4, Maine 9, and US 1.

Southwestern Corner

280 miles ● 2 to 3 days ● Spring through fall. Late fall is the best time for quiet and solitude at Lake Sunapee and Mount Monadnock.

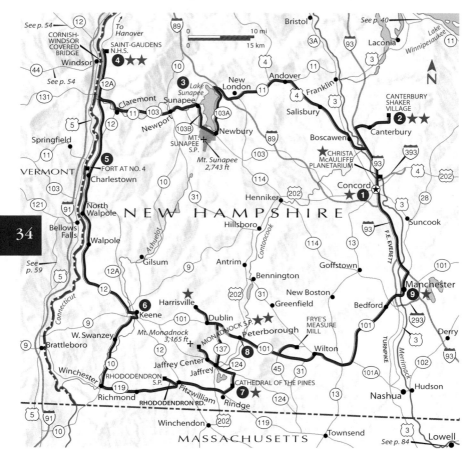

Proud home to New England's longest covered bridge, New Hampshire's southwestern corner also holds the high, lone mountain that gave the world the word "monadnock," and a once mighty base of New England's textile industry. This drive explores a landscape of little known gems.

The route begins in Concord, the state capital, and arcs north and west to popular Lake Sunapee. Striking due west to the Connecticut River Valley, it visits a sculptor's retreat and a reproduction of an early fort. Swinging east through Keene to solitary Monadnock, the state's highest mountain, the drive ends in Manchester, where the power of the Merrimack River produced a river of cotton cloth.

English traders established a post along the banks of the Merrimack in 1660, but it took another 73 years for pioneers from Massachusetts to settle ❶ **Concord**★ *(Chamber of Commerce 603-224-2508)*. In 1816 construction began on the magnificent granite-and-marble **State House** *(107 N. Main St. 603-271-2154. Mon.-Fri.)*, which still crowns the capital city. A self-guided tour of historical Concord begins here. Exhibits at the new **Museum of New Hampshire History**★ *(Hamel Center, Eagle Square. 603-226-3189. Tues.-Sun.; adm. fee)* trace 500 years of the state's evolution.

Not far away, the **League of New Hampshire Craftsmen** *(36 N. Main St. 603-228-8171. Mon.-Sat. year-round, daily during Christmas season)* sells traditional and contemporary handcrafted work by artists and craftspeople.

Two historic houses are also worth a stop. Family furnishings and memorabilia adorn the restored 1838 **Pierce Manse** *(14 Penacook St. 603-224-0094 or 225-2068. Mid-June–Labor Day Mon.-Fri. or by appt.; adm. fee)*, President Franklin Pierce's Concord home between 1842 and 1848. The **Kimball-Jenkins Estate** *(266 N. Main St. 603-225-3932. Mem. Day–Oct. Tues.-Sun.; adm. fee)*, a turn-of-the-century high Victorian Gothic mansion, remained in the same family for 200 years and is filled with their possessions.

35

Hop on I-93 north to I-393 and take the planetarium exit to the pyramid-shaped **Christa McAuliffe Planetarium**★ *(3 Institute Dr. 603-271-STAR. Tues.-Sun. Closed last two weeks in Sept. Reserve ahead; adm. fee)*, named for the New Hampshire teacher-astronaut who died in the 1986 space shuttle *Challenger* disaster. With wraparound sound, multimedia programming, and computer graphics, it's one of the world's most technologically advanced planetariums.

Canterbury Shaker Village, Canterbury

Head north on I-93 to the Canterbury exit and follow signs to the ❷ **Canterbury Shaker Village**★★ *(603-783-*

Dartmouth College

Dartmouth College

A worthwhile side trip north from Claremont follows N.H. 12A and N.H. 10 to Hanover, home of **Dartmouth College,** founded in 1770. Hanover's big town green serves as backdrop for the handsome neoclassical buildings of Dartmouth Row—and for the snow sculptures created each February during Winter Carnival. Places to visit around the green include the **Baker Library** (603-646-2560), whose lower-level reading room features a series of expressionistic murals that trace the conflict of European and indigenous peoples in the Americas. Across the green, the **Hood Museum of Art** (603-646-2808) has a celebrated collection of Assyrian bas-reliefs and of American, European, and ethnographic art.

36

9511. *Daily May-Oct.; April, Nov.-Dec. Fri.-Sun. only; adm. fee).* At its peak in the 1850s, some 300 Shakers lived here in 100 buildings. You'll learn all about the Shaker way of life on the tour of 24 restored structures, where artisans demonstrate such crafts as broommaking and boxmaking. From April through December, the village's Creamery Restaurant serves such Shaker specialties as a New England boiled dinner with salmon and maple-baked beans with smoked ham and brown bread. Candlelight dinners—followed by candlelight tours—are offered on Friday and Saturday nights. Call the village for reservations.

Backtrack one exit south on I-93 and head north then west on US 4 and N.H. 11 to 4,085-acre ❸ **Lake Sunapee** *(Lake Sunapee Business Assoc. 603-763-2495 or 800-258-3530).* N.H. 103A winds south along the lakeshore to the **Fells Historic Site at the John Hay National Wildlife Refuge** *(603-763-5041 or 763-2452. House tours Mem. Day–Columbus Day weekends),* where you can tour the unfurnished, colonial revival house once belonging to Hay, the U.S. secretary of state from 1898 to 1905. The grounds encompass nature trails, formal gardens, and lake views.

Down the road, **Mount Sunapee State Park** *(N.H. 103. 603-763-2356)* has hiking and mountain-biking trails and a lovely beach *(adm. fee).* At the park's ski area, chairlifts *(call for schedule; fare)* transport skiers and summer sightseers to the summit of 2,743-foot **Mount Sunapee.** For nine days every August, some 400 artisans show their work here at the annual **League of New Hampshire Craftsmen's Fair** *(603-224-1471).*

Several companies at **Sunapee**'s harbor, 5 miles north on N.H. 103B, offer cruises around the lake. Head west on N.H. 11/103 through Claremont, then north on N.H. 12A to the **Cornish-Windsor Covered Bridge.** Spanning the Connecticut River and linking New Hampshire to Vermont, it's New England's longest covered bridge at 450 feet.

Just north lies the ❹ **Saint-Gaudens National Historic Site ★ ★** *(603-675-2175. Buildings open Mem. Day–Oct., grounds open year-round. Call for tour schedule; adm. fee),* the home, gardens, and studio of famed sculptor Augustus Saint-Gaudens (1848-1907). Examples of his best known works, including a cast of the Robert Gould Shaw Memorial on Boston Common, stand in the formal gardens he designed and developed. Family possessions fill Aspet, the sculptor's home.

Backtrack on N.H. 12A to N.H. 12 and continue farther south to the reconstructed ❺ **Fort at No. 4** *(N.H. 11, one mile NW of Charlestown. 603-826-5700. Late May–Aug. and mid-Sept.–mid-Oct. Wed.-Mon.; adm. fee).* Built in 1744 to protect New England's northwesternmost English-speaking settlement during the French and Indian wars, the fortified village presents demonstrations and exhibits on the home life and skills of the period.

Farther south the former pottery and glassmaking center of ❻ **Keene** *(Chamber of Commerce 603-352-1303)* claims to have the world's widest paved main street (156 feet). The **Historical Society of Cheshire County** *(246 Main St. 603-352-1895. Mon.-Fri.)* displays Keene glassware and pottery. In 1770 the original trustees of Dartmouth College held their first meeting at the 1762 **Wyman Tavern** *(339 Main St. 603-352-1895. June–Labor Day Thurs.-Sat.; adm. fee),* today furnished as a period home.

Restored brick buildings at Harrisville

The scion of one of Keene's prominent families filled his house with art and oddities collected during his travels around the world. They're on exhibit at his home, now the **Horatio Colony House Museum** *(199 Main St. 603-352-0460. June–mid-Oct. Tues.-Sat., mid-Oct.–May Sat. only).*

N.H. 10 winds south along the Ashuelot River through the Swanzey area—one of the country's densest concentrations of covered bridges. You can pick up a map at the **Swanzey Historical Museum** *(N.H. 10, West Swanzey. 603-352-4579. Mem. Day–foliage season).*

At Winchester, bear left on N.H. 119 and follow Rhododendron Road (just before N.H. 12) north to **Rhododendron State Park** *(603-532-8862. Seasonal; adm. fee).* There's usually something blossoming, but if you can, be here in July when some 16 acres of wild rhododendrons—one of the largest tracts north of the Alleghenies—are in full bloom.

Farther ahead in Fitzwilliam, follow signs for the ❼ **Cathedral of the Pines** ★ *(75 Cathedral Entrance. 603-899-3300. May-Oct.),* overlooking Mount Monadnock.

37

Dedicated to all Americans killed in battle, the outdoor nonsectarian place of prayer and meditation encompasses the Altar of the Nation and the country's first memorial to American women war dead. Scheduled meditations are offered on some summer weekdays.

The drive heads north to N.H. 124 and west through Jaffrey to tiny **Jaffrey Center.** The cemetery next to the 1773 **Meeting House** holds the graves of novelist Willa Cather (1873-1947), a summer visitor for many years, and Amos Fortune, a slave who purchased his freedom in 1769 and settled here. Each summer the **Amos Fortune Forum** *(603-532-4549)* brings prominent speakers to the Meeting House.

Continue through town and follow signs on N.H. 124 to **Monadnock State Park ★ ★** *(603-532-8862. No pets. Adm. fee),* surrounding 3,165-foot **Mount Monadnock.** Most of the 40 miles of hiking trails end up at the rocky, wind-swept summit. Pick up a trail map at the check-in gate.

Return to Jaffrey and go north on N.H. 137, then west on N.H. 101 to Dublin. Just past the tiny traffic island, veer north on New Harrisville Road, which twists and turns for 4 miles to **Harrisville ★.** Described as a miniature version of the textile capital of Lowell, Massachusetts, the village remains the nation's only intact 19th-century textile community. For a walking tour brochure contact **Historic Harrisville, Inc.** *(603-827-3722. P.O. Box 79, Harrisville, N.H. 03450).*

Merrimack River kayaker, Manchester

Backtrack to N.H. 101 and ramble east to the pretty little town of ❽ **Peterborough** *(Chamber of Commerce 603-924-7234),* said to have been the model for Thornton Wilder's play *Our Town.* Peterborough has been a vibrant artistic and cultural community since 1907, when composer Edward MacDowell first invited artists to his woodland home here. In addition to the MacDowell Colony artists retreat, the town is also home of the

Peterborough Players *(Hadley Rd. 603-924-7585)*, a professional summer theater company; and the **New England Marionette Theatre** *(24 Main St. 603-924-4333)*, which presents opera performances on weekends.

A restored mill house, a country store exhibit, and toy and tool collections at the **Peterborough Historical Society and Museum** *(19 Grove St. 603-924-3235. Mon.-Fri.)* help recreate the town's history.

Farther east, at the junction of N.H. 101 and N.H. 45, turn left onto a country road that winds 4 miles to **Frye's Measure Mill** *(12 Frye Mill Rd. 603-654-6581. Mill tours June-Oct. Sat. only, shop open April–mid-Dec. Tues.-Sun.; fee for tours)*. Craftspeople still use the 1858 water-powered sawmill to create colonial and Shaker box reproductions. You can buy one in the museum shop.

The drive continues east and north on N.H. 101 to ❾ **Manchester**★ *(Chamber of Commerce 603-666-6600)*, northern New England's biggest city (pop. 99,570) and, from the mid-19th to early 20th centuries, the world's largest textile producer. In 1935 the **Amoskeag Manufacturing Company**★ closed its doors, leaving empty a mile-long row of redbrick buildings along the Merrimack River. Today the renovated Mill Yard District houses a multitude of smaller businesses and industries, including the **SEE Science Center**★ *(324 Commercial St. 603-669-0400. Daily in summer, rest of year weekends only; adm. fee)*, with more than 70 hands-on learning exhibits. Photos, artifacts, fine and decorative arts, and documents at the **Manchester Historic Association** *(129 Amherst St. 603-622-7531. Tues.-Sat.)* chronicle the city's history. The association also has information on mill tours.

The superb **Currier Gallery of Art**★★ *(201 Myrtle Way. 603-669-6144. Wed.-Mon.; adm. fee)* houses an extensive and eclectic collection that includes art from the 13th through 20th centuries and New Hampshire-made 18th-century furniture. The museum oversees the **Zimmerman House**★ *(603-626-4158. Fri.-Mon.; adm. fee)*, the only New England residence designed by Frank Lloyd Wright that is open to the public. Tours leave by van from the museum. The most in-depth tour, held Saturdays at 2:30 p.m., requires reservations.

The weekend after Labor Day, Manchester hosts the annual **Riverfest** *(Stark Landing. 603-623-2623)*, a three-day waterfront celebration with entertainment, water activities, a Saturday concert, and fireworks.

Lakes Region

**240 miles ● 2 to 3 days ● Late spring through fall ●
The resort towns around Lake Winnipesaukee, particularly Weirs Beach, are crowded on summer weekends.**

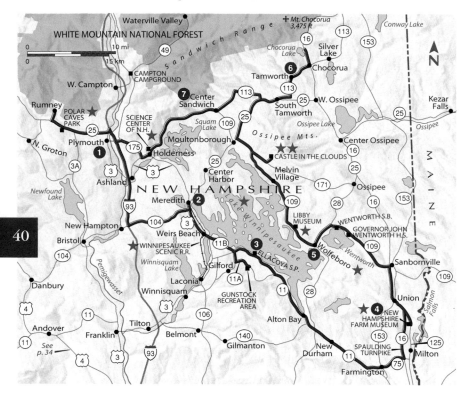

With 283 miles of shoreline and more than 250 islands, Winnipesaukee is New Hampshire's largest lake and one of New England's premier inland summer resorts. But this central region of the Granite State includes hundreds of smaller lakes and ponds, special places where the cry of the loon is more often heard than the roar of motorboats.

Starting northwest of Lake Winnipesaukee at Plymouth, the drive makes a quick side trip to some fascinating caves. It then loops south to Meredith and follows the lake's southwestern shore, where cruise boats head out among wooded islands. After circling through small towns and rolling countryside along the Maine border, the route hugs the lake's northeastern shore, visiting the site of a colonial governor's long-gone mansion and a millionaire's surviving castle. It returns to Plymouth beside quiet Squam Lake.

Fishing from a pier at Weirs Beach

From **❶ Plymouth,** head west on N.H. 25 to **Polar Caves Park★** *(Tenney Mountain Hwy. 603-536-1888 or 800-273-1886. Mid-May–mid-Oct.; adm. fee).* Thousands of years ago, giant blocks of granite cracked and fell in the wake of a receding glacier, creating the caves and passages seen here today.

Farther north in **Rumney** stands the **Mary Baker Eddy House** *(58 Stinson Lake Rd. 603-786-9943. May-Oct. Tues.-Sun.),* where the founder of the Christian Science Church lived between 1860 and 1862. A tour of her earlier dwelling in nearby North Groton starts from here.

Backtrack to Plymouth and take I-93 south to the N.H. 104 exit. Ramble east to US 3, then north a short way to **❷ Meredith,** on the shores of **Lake Winnipesaukee★** *(Lakes Region Assn. 603-253-8555 or 800-60-LAKES).* Hop on the **Winnipesaukee Scenic Railroad★** *(US 3. 603-279-5253. Daily July–Labor Day, Sat.-Sun. Mem. Day–June and Labor Day–Columbus Day; adm. fee)* for a two-hour ride along the lakeshore. (The train also leaves from Weirs Beach.) Beginning in July, dinner trains run on some summer evenings. The **Inn and Marketplace at Mill Falls** *(US 3. 603-279-7006)* surrounds a 19th-century linen mill and a 40-foot waterfall.

From the lively summer tourist mecca of **Weirs Beach** *(Chamber of Commerce 603-524-5531 or 800-531-2347),* a succession of excursion boats named *Mount Washington* have ferried sightseers around the lake since 1872. The current one, 1,250-passenger **M.S. *Mount Washington*★★** *(Lakeside Ave. 603-366-BOAT. May-Oct.; fare),* puts into several ports. The **M.V. *Sophie C.*** *(June-Oct.; fare)* takes passengers

Costumed interpreter at New Hampshire Farm Museum, near Milton

42

on its mail delivery route to some of the islands.

A brief detour on N.H. 11A leads to **Gunstock Recreation Area** *(603-293-4341 ext. 191 or 800-486-7862)*, a year-round resort with a downhill ski area and extensive hiking trails. Ask for a trail map at the campground office and climb to the summit of 1,400-foot **Gunstock Mountain** via the somewhat rigorous, 5-mile round-trip **Brook Trail.** If you want to swim, stop at ❸ **Ellacoya State Park** *(N.H. 11. 603-293-7821. May-Oct.; adm. fee)*, whose 600-foot beach overlooks the Ossipee Mountains and the Sandwich Range.

Continue south to Farmington, then go east on N.H. 75 and north on Spaulding Turnpike (N.H. 16). Take the Union exit to the ❹ **New Hampshire Farm Museum**★ *(N.H. 125. 603-652-7840. Daily mid-June–Labor Day, Labor Day–mid-June Sat.-Sun.; adm. fee)*, which encompasses the Plummer homestead and the Jones farm, an 1890s working farm. You'll also find an old-fashioned country store and blacksmith and cobbler shops.

Proceed north on N.H. 16 and N.H. 109 about 15 miles to the **Governor John Wentworth Historic Site** *(N.H. 109)*. Only a historical marker remains where, in 1768, the state's last royal governor erected a country estate in the wilderness. Farther ahead, take a dip in Lake Wentworth at **Wentworth State Beach** *(603-569-3699. May-Sept.; adm. fee)*.

Several attractions await just up the road in the town of ❺ **Wolfeboro**★ *(Chamber of Commerce 603-569-2200)*, which calls itself "America's first resort." The **Wright Museum**★ *(77 Center St. 603-569-1212. Call for schedule; adm. fee)* re-creates the home front during World War II, with costumes and an extensive collection of operating vintage vehicles. Craftspeople at the **Hampshire Pewter Company** *(43 Mill St. 603-569-4944. Factory tours weekdays Mem. Day–Columbus Day)* create tabletop accessories using colonial-era techniques. The **Wolfeboro Historical Society** *(337 S. Main St. 603-569-4997. July–Labor Day Mon.-Sat. or by appt.)* maintains several buildings, including the circa 1778 **Clark House.**

About 4 miles ahead, the **Libby Museum**★ *(N.H. 109. 603-569-1035. June–mid-Sept. Tues.-Sun.; adm. fee)*, started in 1912 by naturalist Henry Forrest Libby, houses exhibits on mammals, birds, the indigenous Abenaki people, and artifacts from the Governor Wentworth site.

Beyond Melvin Village, take N.H. 171 east to **Castle in the Clouds**★ ★ *(N.H. 171. 603-476-2352 or 800-729-2468. Daily mid-June–mid-Oct., weekends only mid-May–mid-June;*

adm. fee). In 1913 eccentric millionaire Thomas Plant completed construction of this magnificent multimillion-dollar stone castle high above Lake Winnipesaukee. Lunch is available in the carriage house.

The drive continues north on N.H. 25 and N.H. 113 to
❻ Tamworth, home of the **Barnstormers Summer Theatre** *(Main St. 603-323-8500. Call for schedule; fee for performances).* Farther north, in the shadow of 3,475-foot **Mount Chocorua** (see sidebar this page), beautiful **Chocorua Lake** offers a swimming beach at its north end.

Backtrack through Chocorua and follow N.H. 113 west to the village of **❼ Center Sandwich,** where the **League of New Hampshire Craftsmen**★ *(35 Main St. 603-284-6831. Mid-May–mid-Oct.)* sells such crafts as pottery and hand-blown glass. The league, which began here in 1926, also sells hand-crafted works at six other stores across the state.

Farther along, N.H. 113 skirts **Squam Lake,** made famous by the movie *On Golden Pond.* The loons are still here. Several companies in Holderness offer boat tours, including the **Original Golden Pond Tours** *(Holderness Bridge. 603-279-4405. Mem. Day–foliage season Wed.-Mon.; fare)* and **Squam Lake Tours** *(US 3. 603-968-7577. May-Oct.; fare).*

At the southwestern end of Squam Lake, the 200-acre **Science Center of New Hampshire**★ *(N.H. 113. 603-968-7194. May-Oct.; adm. fee)* provides a delightful place to learn about native wildlife and plants. A popular nature trail here winds past more than 30 live animals and hands-on activities, and another climbs atop a 1,067-foot mountain. In summer, naturalists offer trailside mini-talks.

A Mighty Curse

Mount Chocorua is named for a Pequawket chief who lived near Conway about 1760. One version of a legend has it that his son died after drinking poison that a white settler named Cornelius Campbell had put out for foxes. In retaliation, the chief killed Campbell's family. Campbell pursued the chief up to a precipice on the mountain's summit and demanded that he fling himself into the abyss. Staring down the barrel of the settler's musket, Chocorua saw no way to escape. In defiance, he leveled a withering curse upon the white race: "May lightning blast your crops. . . . winds and fire destroy your dwellings. . . . wolves fatten upon your bones." Then Chocorua leaped to his death.

43

Sunrise at Quincy Bog, near Rumney

White Mountains ★★

**130 miles ● Half to full day ● Spring through fall
● Roads crowded on fall foliage weekends.**

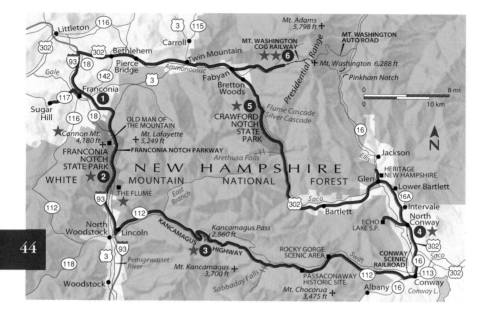

Central New Hampshire's White Mountains form the
rooftop of New England. Here, 6,288-foot Mount Washington, the Northeast's highest peak, crowns the majestic Presidential Range. Much of this sparsely populated region
comprises the nearly 800,000-acre White Mountain National
Forest, parts of which are preserved as wilderness.

Starting in Franconia, the drive heads south through
Franconia Notch, one of three great White Mountain
passes. At Lincoln, it picks up the Kancamagus Highway
and winds east into the heart of the mountains to Conway. Returning to Franconia, the route cuts through
Crawford Notch and offers occasional views of noble
Mount Washington.

In ❶ **Franconia** a narrow dirt road leads to the battered
mailbox marking the **Frost Place** ★ *(Ridge Rd., off N.H. 116.
603-823-5510. Mem. Day–June Sat.-Sun. p.m., July–mid-Oct. Wed.-
Mon. p.m.; adm. fee).* Poet Robert Frost, a 25-year, on-and-off
inhabitant of this simple 1859 farmhouse, once proclaimed,
"I choose to be a plain New Hampshire farmer." His house
is now a museum, with first editions, memorabilia, and a
resident poet who gives readings during a midsummer
poetry festival. Take the half-mile poetry-nature trail for a

Old Man of the Mountain,
Franconia Notch State Park

delightful stroll through the woods that inspired Frost. On a more prosaic note, **Polly's Pancake Parlor** *(N.H. 117, Sugar Hill. 603-823-5575. Daily mid-May–mid-Oct., Sat.-Sun. April–mid-May and mid-Oct.–Nov.)*, a local institution since the Depression, serves its famous pancakes all day.

South of town, I-93 merges with the nearly 9-mile **Franconia Notch Parkway,** cutting through Franconia Notch. This scenic stretch of highway abounds in natural attractions, many preserved within 6,440-acre ❷ **Franconia Notch State Park★** *(603-823-5563)*. On a clear day you can see almost forever from atop 4,180-foot **Cannon Mountain★**—or at least to Vermont and Maine. **Cannon Mountain Aerial Tramway** *(603-823-5563. Mid-May–Oct.; adm. fee)* is the quickest way to the summit, where a walking trail ends at an observation tower. At the mountain's base, the **New England Ski Museum** *(603-823-7177. Mid-May–mid-Oct. and Dec.-March)* traces the history of the sport.

Cannon Mountain's aerial tram

Farther south, stop at **Profile Lake**—called the Old Man's Washbowl—for a great view of a natural formation known as the **Old Man of the Mountain.** Just ahead lies one of the area's most spectacular natural sites: the **Flume★** *(603-745-8391. Mid-May–Oct.; adm. fee)*, a 180-million-year-old natural gorge whose granite walls rise up to 90 feet. In their shadow, boardwalks and paths crisscross picturesque Flume Brook. In summer you can travel by shuttle bus from the Visitor Center to the Flume entrance, or walk the 0.7-mile trail. Arrive early to avoid the crowds.

Just outside Lincoln, pick up the ❸ **Kancamagus Highway★,** a National Forest Scenic Byway that meanders east for 34.5 miles through pristine wilderness. Punctuated by pullouts, picnic areas, and hiking trails, the road climbs to nearly 3,000 feet as it traverses the flank of **Mount Kancamagus.** Along the way, take the short Sabbaday Brook Trail to **Sabbaday Falls,** whose three separate drops tumble 25 feet over a wall of granite. The early 1800s Russell Colbath Historic Homestead at the **Passaconaway Historic Site** *(603-447-5448. Daily July-Sept., call for Oct. hours)* provides insight into the lives of the early settlers here, as well as interesting local lore. The Swift River forms natural ponds at the **Rocky Gorge Scenic Area,** making it a perfect place to cool off on a summer's day. (Be sure to swim at designated locations, as river currents can be dangerous.)

Turning north on N.H. 16, head past the myriad outlet stores in Conway to ❹ **North Conway**★ *(Chamber of Commerce 603-356-5701 or 800-367-3364).* Check the weather conditions atop Mount Washington at the **Mount Washington Observatory Resource Center** *(2448 Main St. 603-356-8345. Mid-May–mid-Oct.).* For a nostalgic ride back to the era of steam and early diesel locomotive travel, hop aboard the **Conway Scenic Railroad** *(38 Norcross Circle. 603-356-5251. Mid-April–mid-Dec.; adm. fee),* which leaves from the 1874 mansard-roofed Victorian train station.

For panoramic views, drive to the top of 700-foot Cathedral Ledge in **Echo Lake State Park** *(2 miles W of N.H. 16, off River Rd. 603-356-2672. Mem. Day–Labor Day).* In **Intervale,** railroad buffs will want to stop at the **Hartmann Model Railroad & Toy Museum** *(N.H. 16/US 302. 603-356-9922. Adm. fee).* Operating model train layouts from large to small scale are displayed in more than 5,000 feet of exhibit space.

Just north of the N.H. 16–US 302 junction in **Glen, Heritage New Hampshire** *(603-383-9776. Mid-May–mid-Oct.; adm. fee)* reviews the state's history from 1634 to the present. Visitors are transported back in time on a mock 17th-century sea voyage, then guided through numerous exhibits that re-create the colonial through modern eras. The costumed guides, enthusiastic and

Silver Cascade in Crawford Notch State Park

knowledgeable amateur historians, enhance the experience. The 6-mile stretch of US 302 through ❺ **Crawford**

Notch State Park★ *(603-374-2272)* offers spectacular views of the southern reaches of the Presidential Range, including **Mount Washington.** Take the moderately steep, 1.3-mile hike to **Arethusa Falls,** the state's highest at 200 feet. Farther along, watch for several waterfalls visible from the highway, including **Silver Cascade.**

Mount Washington Hotel, Bretton Woods

In **Bretton Woods** the great white confection with the bright red roof is the **Mount Washington Hotel**★ *(603-278-1000 or 800-258-0330. Call for tour schedule),* built by railroad tycoon Joseph Stickney in 1902. Modeled after a luxury cruise ship, the lavish European-style spa turned Bretton Woods into a well-known resort. You can see the craftsmanship of the 250 Italian artisans who helped build the hotel in the Grand Ballroom's elaborate plasterwork and stuccoed walls. History was made at the hotel when the World Bank and the International Monetary Fund were founded at a 1944 conference.

With its toothed-cog gears, rack rails, and valiant little locomotives, the nearby ❻ **Mount Washington Cog Railway**★★ *(Off US 302, E of Fabyan. 603-278-5404 or 800-922-8825. May-Oct. Reserve ahead; fare)* was an engineering marvel when it started operation in 1869. Today, its relentless climb to the top of Mount Washington still seems miraculous. The antique engines belch and snort up the 3-mile route, at one point climbing a 37-percent grade called Jacob's Ladder. At the summit is the **Mount Washington Observatory** *(603-356-8345. Open to members only, but worth joining for tour of weather room; fee for museum)* and its museum, which keeps scientific information on the mountain's meteorology, geology, and botany. Don't be disappointed if the summit is socked in by clouds—it's that way 60 percent of the time.

At the turn of the century, the pure air of **Bethlehem,** farther west on US 302, attracted hay fever sufferers, and the place became a thriving resort. Tag a tree at the **Rocks Christmas Tree Farm** *(US 302. 603-444-6228 or 800-639-5373)* in autumn, and the Society for the Protection of New Hampshire Forests will ship it to you for a fee.

Snug Huts

For over a hundred years, hikers in the White Mountains have been welcomed to a string of snug huts operated by the Appalachian Mountain Club. Founded in 1876 by a group of outdoorsmen who had enjoyed a similar system in the Swiss Alps, the huts are mostly located about a day's walk apart. The system counts eight huts, plus two additional overnight facilities—at the Pinkham Notch Visitor Center on N.H. 16 and at the Crawford Notch hostel on US 302. Reservations are a must for overnight guests, who are given dinner, breakfast, a blanket, and a bunk. In the morning, it's back on the trail to the next hut. For information, call the Appalachian Mountain Club *(603-466-2727)*.

**240 miles ● 2 to 3 days ● Late spring through mid-fall
● Except near Lake Champlain, foliage peaks a week
or two earlier than in the southern parts of the state—
usually around late September and the first week
of October. The road through Smugglers Notch (Vt. 108)
is closed from first snowfall to spring.**

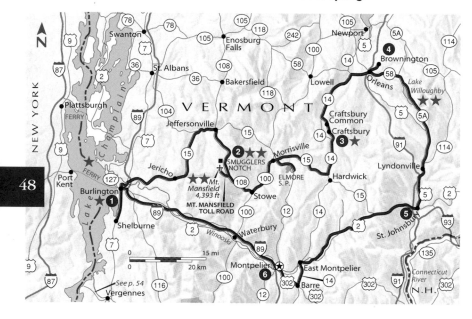

It's almost as if Vermont grows more expansive in the counties closest to Canada. Here you find the state's capital and largest city, its highest mountain and the widest part of Lake Champlain. This jaunt takes in the mountains and the valleys, the cities and the small towns; along the way, it stops at a superb museum of Americana, the world's largest granite quarry, and an ice-cream mecca.

Beginning in Burlington on Lake Champlain, the drive heads east beneath the brow of Mount Mansfield. It then wends north along the fringes of the remote Northeast Kingdom—Vermont's northeasternmost counties—and reaches St. Johnsbury by way of peaceful villages and a gemlike lake cradled by mountains. Heading west again, the drive visits the granite capital of Barre and the state capital of Montpelier before returning to Burlington.

Dubbed the Queen City back when it commanded a trading center on Lake Champlain, ❶ **Burlington** ★ *(Chamber of Commerce 802-863-3489)* today bustles as a university town. Its downtown centerpiece is the **Church Street Mall,** a pedestrian-only avenue of shops, restaurants, and sidewalk cafés ending at the beautiful 1816 **First Unitarian Universalist Church** *(802-862-5630)*. Uphill lies the campus of the **University of Vermont** *(Information Office 802-656-3480. Mon.-Fri.)*, centered on a green lined with fine old buildings, including a

View of Grand Isle in Lake Champlain

student center designed by Henry Hobson Richardson and built in 1885. Displays at the university's **Fleming Museum** *(Colchester Ave. 802-656-2090. Tues.-Sun.; adm. fee)* include American and European paintings, ethnographic materials, and an Egyptian mummy.

Burlington's lakefront has walking and biking trails, a park and marina, and the new **Lake Champlain Basin Science Center** *(1 College St. 802-864-1848. Daily mid-June–Labor Day, rest of year weekends only; adm. fee)*, which focuses on the ecology, history, and culture of the lake and environs. Kids will enjoy the hands-on "Secrets of the Lake" exhibit. At the nearby King Street dock, catch the **ferry★** to Port Kent, N.Y. *(Lake Champlain Ferries 802-864-9804. Late spring–mid-fall; fare)*; the two-hour round-trip offers incomparable mountain and lake scenery. Or cruise and dine on the luxurious ***Spirit of Ethan Allen II*** *(Lake Champlain Shoreline Cruises. Burlington Boathouse, foot of College St. 802-862-8300. Mid-May–Oct.; fare)*.

North of downtown, the **Ethan Allen Homestead** *(Vt. 127. 802-865-4556. Daily in summer; call for spring and fall schedule; adm. fee)* is a restoration of the farmhouse where the leader of the Green Mountain Boys lived his last two

---

The Islands

When you hear a Vermonter talking about "the islands," they're probably referring to the state's own freshwater archipelago. The **Lake Champlain islands** *(Chamber of Commerce 802-372-5683)* are connected by causeway with the mainland, just a few miles north of Burlington via I-89 and US 2. A world apart, the islands combine rolling dairy lands and orchards with splendid views of the lake, the Green Mountains, and New York State's Adirondacks. Along or near US 2, several fine state parks offer camping, swimming, and fishing. There's also the 1783 **Hyde Log Cabin,** Vermont's oldest; the summer home of Austria's famous **Royal Lipizzan Stallions;** the **Ed Weed Fish Culture Station,** a state-of-the-art hatchery for trout and salmon; and, on Isle La Motte, **St. Anne Shrine,** built on the site of Vermont's first French settlement (1666).

49

years (1787-89). Exhibits and a multimedia show trace Allen's career and the region's history.

Detour south from Burlington on US 7 to reach **Shelburne** and the **Shelburne Museum**★★ *(802-985-3346. Daily late May–Oct., by guided tour only rest of year; adm. fee)*, a 45-acre trove of Americana that stands as a monument to founder Electra Havemeyer Webb's passion for collecting. The museum's holdings include entire structures, such as a lighthouse, a one-room schoolhouse, and a covered bridge, as well as galleries filled with quilts, farm tools, carriages, paintings, cigar-store Indians—everything that was vital or ornamental in preindustrial America. Don't miss the steamboat *Ticonderoga,* brought to dry land here after its lake days ended. Another Webb family legacy awaits at nearby **Shelburne Farms**★ *(102 Harbor Rd. 802-985-8686. Open daily, guided tours mid-May–mid-Oct.; adm. fee)*, a 1,400-acre lakeside center for agricultural and environmental education, with miles of walking trails. In the magnificently restored barn, you can visit the Children's Farmyard and watch cheese being made. Also on the premises, the turn-of-the-century **Inn at Shelburne Farms**★ *(802-985-8498. Mid-May–mid-Oct.)* offers superlative lodging and dining.

Head back into Burlington on US 7 and follow Vt. 15 east to **Jericho.** Here, the roadside **Old Red Mill** *(Vt. 15. 802-899-3225. Daily in summer; call for winter schedule)* once ground flour; today, it houses a craft shop and small museum focusing on the career of native W.A. "Snowflake" Bentley, who in the late 1800s first recorded the wondrous crystalline patterns of snowflakes with microscope and camera.

Log cabin interior, Shelburne Museum

Continue on Vt. 15 to Jeffersonville and take Vt. 108 south as it climbs up 2,160-foot ❷ **Smugglers Notch**★★ *(Road closed from first snowfall to spring)*. From the small parking area at the crest of the shadowy, steep-walled notch, rugged trails lead to higher elevations, including the 4,393-foot summit of **Mount Mansfield**★★, the roof of Vermont. Drive down sharply elbowing curves to the other side of the notch to reach two easier ways to the top—the **Stowe Mountain**

Resort Gondola ★
(Vt. 108. 802-253-3000. Mid-June–Oct. and ski season; fare. Dinner reservations required at Cliff House restaurant on summit),
with its enclosed, eight-passenger cars suspended by cable, and the **Mount Mansfield Toll Road** *(Vt. 108. 802-253-3000. Late May–Oct.; adm. fee),* a breathtaking auto route to the mountain's southern summit, or "nose."

Mount Mansfield

Vt. 108 descends into **Stowe** *(Visitor Center 802-253-7321 or 800-24-STOWE),* oldest of Vermont's big ski resorts. The village itself is tiny, barely more than three blocks long, but it has a fine recreation path—a paved, motor-free 11-mile round-trip route through the country, favored by cross-country skiers, runners, walkers, cyclists, and rollerbladers.

Take Vt. 100 north to Morrisville, then detour south on Vt. 12 a few miles to **Elmore State Park** *(802-888-2982. Mem. Day–Labor Day; adm. fee).* Swim or rent a canoe at Lake Elmore, or climb the fire tower atop Elmore Mountain for views that encompass the lake below, Mount Mansfield to the west, and New Hampshire's Mount Washington to the east.

Back in Morrisville, the drive heads east on Vt. 15 toward the Northeast Kingdom, a hilly corner of Vermont known for its bucolic charm. In Hardwick, take Vt. 14 north and watch for a paved road on the right that leads to the hill town of ❸ **Craftsbury** ★. The **Craftsbury Inn** *(802-586-2848)* offers good food and lodgings. Two hundred years old and as fresh as its white paint is the part of town called **Craftsbury Common.** Its lovely green, site of the posh **Inn on the Common** *(802-586-9619),* seems to float on a high ridge above the valley.

Bear left north of Craftsbury Common to return to Vt. 14 north, then head east on Vt. 58 through Orleans

Autumn along Vt. 108

and watch for signs to **4** **Brownington.** The town's **Old Stone House Museum** *(802-754-2022. Daily July and Aug., late spring and early fall Fri.-Tues.; adm. fee)* was built as a secondary school dormitory in 1834-36 by the Rev. Alexander Twilight, a local schoolmaster and possibly America's first black college graduate. The massive stone structure now holds the collections of the Orleans County Historical Society, an antiquarian's delight. Next door, you can stroll the formal garden at the 1834 **Cyrus Eaton House.** A meadowlike park across the road culminates at the **Prospect Hill Observatory,** a raised viewing platform that commands vistas of Jay Peak, Lake Memphremagog, and distant Quebec.

Return to Vt. 58 and follow it east to Vt. 5A, then head south along the eastern shore of **Lake Willoughby**★★. Mountains rise sharply from either shore, giving the 5-mile-long lake a dramatic fjordlike appearance.

Continue south on Vt. 5A to US 5, which leads south through Lyndonville to the historic redbrick railroad city of **5** **St. Johnsbury.** Here Thaddeus Fairbanks invented the platform scale, and Fairbanks family philanthropy stands behind the **Fairbanks Museum and Planetarium** *(Main and Prospect Sts. 802-748-2372. Museum open all year; planetarium open daily July-Aug., rest of year weekends only; separate adm. fees).* Housed in a Romanesque Revival building, the museum provides a Victorian slant on natural history—lots of mounted animals and birds—but it also displays Native American and Asian ethnographic holdings and lots of Vermontiana . . . plus a few scales. The planetarium is a trifle small but fun. Just down the street you'll find another Fairbanks bequest, the **St. Johnsbury Athenaeum and Art Gallery**★ *(30 Main St. 802-748-8291. Mon.-Sat.).* In the rear of the athenaeum, or public library, the wall-size "Domes of the Yosemite" by Albert Bierstadt dominates the gallery of canvases by 19th-century European academicians and American luminists.

East of downtown, the **Maple Grove Museum and Factory** *(167 Portland St. 802-748-5141. Museum and gift shop open daily late May–Oct.; factory tours Mon.-Fri. all year; adm. fee)* reveals the time-honored intricacies that go into creating

St. Johnsbury Art Gallery

Vermont's signature flavor. The sugaring season takes place only in springtime, but you can see the boiling process here year-round. The shop sells maple sugar in all its permutations.

Take US 2 west out of town. At East Montpelier follow Vt. 14 south into the city of **Barre** (pronounced BARE-ie), whose foremost industry is on display at **Hope Cemetery** *(Vt. 14. Mon.-Fri.)*. Local craftspeople have fashioned Barre granite into a variety of fantastic monuments. Look for an easy chair, a soccer ball, and the pensive likeness of a local labor leader. South of town at **Rock of Ages Quarry** ★ *(773 Graniteville Rd. 802-476-3121. Walking tours daily May-Oct.; shuttle tours June–mid-Oct. Mon.-Sat.; fare for shuttle tour)* stonecutters hew enormous blocks of stone from sheer walls that descend deep into Barre's granite deposits. See the granite cut and carved at the **Craftsman Center** *(802-476-3115)*, a mile from the quarry.

It's a short trip west on US 302 to ❻ **Montpelier,** the state capital. Topped by a statue of a goddess symbolizing agriculture, the granite Greek Revival **State House** *(115 State St. 802-828-2228. Tours July–mid-Oct. Mon.-Sat.)* has a spacious, restored Victorian interior that serves as a backdrop for portraits of Vermont heroes and Civil War battle flags. Still, the building has an intimacy befitting a small, rural state, with legislators milling about the halls. Just two doors down, exhibits at the **Vermont Historical Society** *(109 State St. 802-828-2291. Tues.-Sun.; adm. fee)* tell the state's long story. Nearby on the Vermont College campus, the **TW Wood Gallery & Arts Center** *(College Hall, College St. 802-828-8743. Tues.-Sun.; adm. fee)*, founded by Montpelier artist Thomas Waterman Wood more than a century ago, exhibits Wood's own genre paintings and other works.

The drive returns to Burlington via I-89. Along the way, detour north on Vt. 100 to **Ben and Jerry's** *(Waterbury. 802-244-8687. Adm. fee)*. The big ice-cream factory offers tours, samples, and a dessert parlor, and tells you everything you wanted to know about two Long Island guys who became Vermont icons. Continue a couple miles north on Vt. 100 to the **Cold Hollow Cider Mill** *(Waterbury Ctr. 802-244-8771)*, where you can watch cider pressing and buy apple cider, pie, butter, sauce, and even things not made from apples.

53

Cold Hollow Cider Mill, Waterbury Center

260 miles ● 2 to 3 days ● All year ● Many attractions are closed in winter, but snow brings a special beauty to Vermont's landscape. Though roads are well maintained, be sure to allow extra travel time.

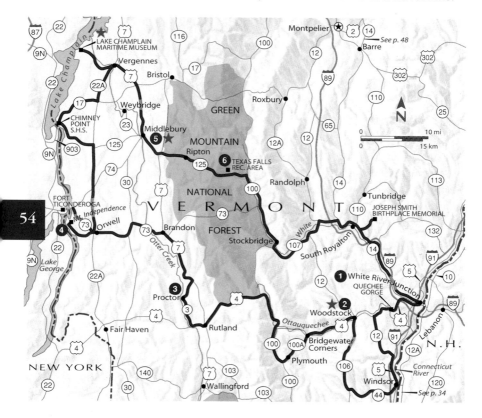

54

The sizable swath of central Vermont traversed on this drive extends from the Connecticut River Valley to the southern shores of Lake Champlain, New England's largest lake. In between, the route crosses the densely wooded heights of the Green Mountains. Sights along the way include a village that gave America a President, the foundations of a lakeside Revolutionary fort, and a home of Vermont's state animal—the Morgan horse.

Beginning at White River Junction, the drive visits genteel Woodstock and Calvin Coolidge's rustic Plymouth Notch before crossing the Green Mountains to Proctor. Continuing north through Champlain Valley dairy lands, the route skirts the lake and angles south and east through the college town of Middlebury. It then climbs into the Green Mountain National Forest and descends along the White River Valley back to its starting point.

❶ White River Junction *(Chamber of Commerce 802-295-6000)* stands near the point where I-91 and I-89 converge, but the town got its name back in railroad days. As a reminder of the steam era, a vintage Boston and Maine 4-4-0 locomotive sits at trackside downtown. Nowadays, White River Junction is in the beer business—the **Catamount Brewing Company** *(58 S. Main St. 802-296-2248. Daily July-Oct., rest of year Sat. only)* gives tours of the beer-making process.

Take US 4 west to the high bridge that spans the Ottauquechee River, and park to peer into forbidding 165-foot **Quechee Gorge.** You'll find picnic tables and hiking trails alongside Vermont's deepest chasm, carved over the past 12,000 years by the swift waters of the Ottauquechee.

Beyond the gorge, turn south onto Vt. 12 to pick up US 5 south into **Windsor,** billed as the "birthplace of Vermont." The claim dates back to the 1777 adoption of a constitution for the independent Republic of Vermont (in existence until statehood in 1791) by representatives gathered at the Elijah West Tavern. Moved a short distance from its original site and renamed the **Old Constitution House** *(N. Main St. 802-828-3051. Late May–mid-Oct.)*, the old tavern showcases historical items including the table on which the constitution is believed to have been drafted. You can see revolutionary developments of a different sort at the **American Precision Museum** *(S. Main St. 802-674-5781. Late May–Oct.; adm. fee)*, located nearby in a mid-19th-century brick factory on the banks of Mill Brook. The museum's vast collection of intricate machine tools document a century and a half of American industrial innovation.

Examine a simpler but no less important technology at the 1866 **Cornish-Windsor Covered Bridge;** at 450 feet, it's New England's longest covered bridge. Sturdy as ever, it carries cars across the Connecticut River to New Hampshire.

Cornish-Windsor Covered Bridge

55

Billings Farm & Museum, Woodstock

Take Vt. 44 west from Windsor, then Vt. 106 north to ❷ **Woodstock**★ *(Chamber of Commerce 802-457-3555),* the birthplace of Vermont's first ski tow. The gracious **Woodstock Inn** *(14 The Green. 802-457-1100 or 800-448-7900)* typifies the elegant community's charms. The **Billings Farm & Museum**★ *(Vt. 12. 802-457-2355. Daily May-Oct., Nov.-Dec. weekends only; adm. fee)* vividly chronicles rural 19th-century life with exhibits of farm tools and an 1890s farmhouse; it also keeps working farm animals—horses, oxen, sheep, and more.

Drive west out of town on US 4, and at Bridgewater Corners branch south onto Vt. 100A to Plymouth and the **Plymouth Notch Historic District**★ *(802-672-3773. Daily Mem. Day–Columbus Day, small exhibits open weekdays rest of year; adm. fee).* Not just the birthplace of President Calvin Coolidge, but the entire hamlet of Plymouth Notch—where he grew up—is preserved as a tribute to the 30th President's career and the Yankee sensibilities that molded him. The tour includes his father's store and the house where the elder Coolidge swore in his son when word came of

Calvin Coolidge Homestead, Plymouth Notch

President Warren G. Harding's death on August 3, 1923. Learn about the Coolidge era in an exhibit hall, wander through a barn filled with carriages and sleighs, and sample cheese made at the factory still owned by Coolidge's son.

Continue south on Vt. 100A, then pick up Vt. 100 north to where it joins US 4, and head west through Rutland to Vt. 3. Meandering north, cross over the marble bridge to ❸ **Proctor,** site of the **Vermont Marble Exhibit** *(62 Main St. 802-459-2300. Mon.-Sat.; adm. fee).* Near quarries that form the center of the state's marble industry, the exhibit showcases beautifully carved and polished marble alongside displays on the stone's hewing and processing. Also in Proctor you'll find **Wilson Castle** *(W. Proctor Rd. 802-773-3284. Mid-May–mid-Oct.; adm. fee),* an 1867 brick mansion (it's a "castle" only by Vermont standards), sumptuously decorated with frescoes, mahogany paneling, Tiffany glass, and European antiques.

Continue north on Vt. 3 to US 7, which leads farther north to **Brandon.** Here, the **Vermont Ski Museum** *(US 7, on the grounds of the Brandon Inn. 802-247-8080. Summer and fall Fri.-Sun.; call for winter hours; adm. fee)* celebrates over 60 years of Vermont skiing in its collections of ski equipment and memorabilia, including many items used by Olympians who trained in the Green Mountains.

From Brandon, head west on Vt. 73 to reach the Champlain Valley town of **Orwell,** set amid dairy farms and apple orchards. Just west of town, Catfish Bay Road wanders to ❹ **Mount Independence** *(802-948-2650 in season, 802-759-2412 rest of year. Grounds open all year. Interpretive Center open Wed.-Sun. Mem. Day–Columbus Day; adm. fee for center).* The Revolutionary-era fort that guarded the southern end of Lake Champlain against British incursions from the north is long gone, but trails along the heights above the lake reveal foundation remnants, and exhibits and artifacts at the new interpretive center recount the story. To catch a tour boat *(802 897-5331. Summer; fare)* to historic **Fort Ticonderoga** *(518-585-2821. May-Oct.; adm. fee)* across the lake, backtrack toward Orwell and take Vt. 73 west.

57

Stained-glass window,
Wilson Castle, Proctor

The main route returns to Orwell, then follows Vt. 22A north and Vt. 125 west to **Chimney Point.** The lakeside **Chimney Point State Historic Site** *(Vt. 125 at Chimney Point Bridge. 802-759-2412. Mem. Day–Columbus Day Wed.-Sun.; adm. fee)* offers insight into the Native American and French heritage of the Champlain Valley and of Vermont.

North from Chimney Point via Vt. 17 and Vt. 22A, **Vergennes**—measuring just one square mile—is Vermont's smallest chartered city. Follow signs leading west from town to the **Lake Champlain Maritime Museum** ★ *(Basin Harbor Rd. 802-475-2022. May–mid-Oct.; adm. fee),* where a splendid collection of watercraft tells about navigation on the big lake from Indian times to the 20th century, with special emphasis on naval battles and the steamboat era.

Back in Vergennes, head south on US 7 to ❺ **Middlebury** ★ *(Chamber of Commerce 802-388-7951),* an archetypal New England college town. Middlebury College's **Museum of Art** *(Center for the Arts 802-388-3711 ext. 5007. Closed during college vacations)* includes a unique collection of Fabergé objects. Downtown Middlebury clusters around the graceful, spired 1809 **Middlebury Congregational Church** *(802-388-7634. Open Sundays, call for tour information),* often cited as Vermont's most beautiful church. The town also offers the **Sheldon Museum** *(1 Park St. 802-388-2117. Mon.-Fri.; adm. fee),* an 1829 mansion filled with 19th-century Vermont furniture, housewares, and paraphernalia; and the **Vermont Folklife Center** *(2 Court St. 802-388-4964. Mem. Day–mid-Oct. Mon.-Sat., rest of year Mon.-Fri.),* where a series of changing exhibits interpret Vermont folkways through arts, crafts, storytelling, and other traditions. In Frog Hollow, a quaint little quarter near Otter Creek Falls, the **Vermont State Craft Center** *(1 Mill St. 802-388-3177)* sells the crafts themselves: ceramics, furniture, jewelry, glassware, and other handwork by state artisans.

Detour north on Vt. 23 toward Weybridge and follow the signs to see fine examples of Vermont's state animal at the **University of Vermont Morgan Horse Farm** *(Horse Farm Rd. 802-388-2011. May-Oct.; adm. fee).*

Autumn in South Royalton

From Middlebury, the drive ambles south on US 7, then east on Vt. 125. Just beyond the town of Ripton, you'll come to the **Robert Frost Interpretive Trail.** Traversing meadow, forest, and marsh, the mile-long trail honors Frost, a one-time Ripton resident, with passages from his poems mounted on plaques along the way. Farther east, the road winds across 2,149-foot **Middlebury Gap** in the Green Mountain National Forest. Watch for signs to the ❻ **Texas Falls Recreation Area** *(802-767-4261).* The falls churn and cascade from pool to pool through a deep cleft in a rocky mountainside, with a trail running alongside.

Vt. 125 ends at Vt. 100, just ahead. Continue south on Vt. 100 to Stockbridge, then head east on Vt. 107 to **South Royalton,** where fine Victorian buildings cluster around a downtown park. From here follow Vt. 14 south to the turnoff for the **Joseph Smith Birthplace Memorial** *(Dairy Hill Rd. 802-763-7742).* A monument and interpretive center mark the 1805 birthplace of the founder of the Church of Jesus Christ of Latter-day Saints.

The drive returns to White River Junction via Vt. 14 and US 5.

150 miles ● 2 to 3 days ● All year; winter scenery fine, but many attractions open spring through fall only ● Fall foliage season, which peaks in early to mid-October, brings the most travelers; plan weekday leaf-peeping trips whenever possible.

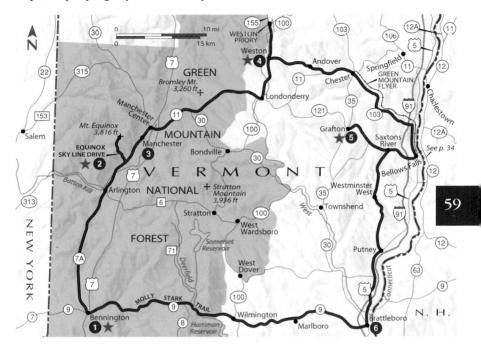

This jaunt around southern Vermont links traditional resort villages with the vibrant larger towns of Bennington and Brattleboro; and rolling dairy lands with rugged, forested mountain terrain, much of it preserved as part of the Green Mountain National Forest.

Begin the drive at the college town of Bennington and head north through Norman Rockwell's Arlington to the ski and shopping capital of Manchester. Cutting across the high country of the national forest, the route descends toward the Connecticut River Valley before meandering south to Brattleboro, with a side trip to the restored hill village of Grafton. The last portion of the drive follows the scenic Molly Stark Trail westward across the state.

❶ **Bennington** ★ *(Chamber of Commerce 802-447-3311)*, the home of small, liberal arts Bennington College, was one of Vermont's earliest settlements (1761) and a haunt of Ethan Allen and his Green Mountain Boys. In the part of town called Old Bennington stands the graceful 1805 **Old First Church** *(Monument Ave.)*, a Palladian gem with a fine open belfry. Behind the church, at the tree-shaded **Old Burying Ground,** the most famous grave belongs to Vermont's laureate, Robert Frost. "I had a lover's quarrel with the world," his tombstone proclaims. Another American icon is well remembered at the **Bennington Museum**★ *(W. Main St. 802-447-1571. Adm. fee)*, which houses the largest public collection of the paintings of Grandma Moses (1860-1961), who lived and worked nearby. Other museum holdings spotlight regional history and decorative arts, including traditional Bennington pottery. The nearby **Bennington Potters** *(324 County St. 802-447-7531)* sells the sturdy, utilitarian ceramic pieces.

Bennington's greatest event actually took place just across the border in New York State, but the **Bennington Battle Monument** *(15 Monument Circle. 802-447-0550. Mid-Apr.–Oct.; adm. fee)* stands squarely in Vermont. With superb views from its top, the 306-foot obelisk commemorates the American victory over the British in the 1777 Battle of Bennington. Nearby, the 35-room, mansard-roofed **Park-McCullough House** *(Park and West Sts. 802-442-5441. Late May–Oct.; adm. fee)* was built in 1865 by descendants of a family that originally settled the site. The clan—with two Vermont governors—never got rid of any of its sumptuous furnishings.

Rockwell model Roy Crofit, Norman Rockwell Exhibition, Arlington

The drive heads north from Bennington on Vt. 7A (also known as Historic 7A) to **Arlington** *(Chamber of Commerce 802-375-2800)*, just the sort of archetypal New England town that would appeal to Norman Rockwell. The illustrator did in fact live here for 14 years, and he used some 200 local residents as models. Fine reproductions hang in the **Norman Rockwell Exhibition** at the Arlington Gallery *(Vt. 7A/Main St. 802-375-6423. Adm. fee)*, where several of the models work as hosts.

Some 4 miles north of Arlington on Vt. 7A you'll see the left-hand turnoff for 6-mile ❷ **Equinox Sky Line Drive**★ *(802-362-1114. May-Oct.; toll)*, which twists and elbows its way to the top of 3,816-foot Mount Equinox. At the top are spectacular views (sometimes as far as New

Hampshire and Maine), hiking trails, and the 20-room **Equinox Mountain Inn** *(802-362-1113. May-Oct. Thurs.-Tues.),* which defines the idea of getting away from it all.

Just ahead on Vt. 7A, ❸ **Manchester** *(Chamber of Commerce 802-362-2100)* has lured sojourners for well over a century. Many of them have stayed—and still do—at the

Hildene, Robert Todd Lincoln house, Manchester

rambling, grandly colonnaded **Equinox** *(Vt. 7A. 802-362-4700 or 800-453-7629),* now restored to its former luxury. Some summer people, though, preferred to build their own retreats, among them Robert Todd Lincoln, the President's son. His Georgian Revival **Hildene** ★ *(Vt. 7A. 802-362-1788. Mid-May–Oct. and Christmas week; adm. fee),* built in 1903-05, stayed in the family until 1975. Be sure to walk around the gorgeously landscaped grounds.

Long before it cast its lot with a raft of upscale factory outlets, Manchester was famous for its location on the **Batten Kill,** one of America's premier trout streams. The Batten Kill explains the site of the **Orvis Company** *(Vt. 7A. 802-362-3622. Three-day fly-fishing courses offered),* manufacturer of famous fly rods that shoppers can test on the company's own stocked pond, and the **American Museum of Fly Fishing** *(Vt. 7A. 802-362-3300. Daily May-Oct., rest of year closed weekends; adm. fee),* where exhibits trace the sport's development and showcase the tackle of such celebrities as Ernest Hemingway and Bing Crosby.

Head east from Manchester Center on Vt. 11/30 and begin the climb past the ski slopes of **Bromley Mountain** and views of the more distant trails of Stratton Mountain. At Londonderry, turn north on Vt. 100 to ❹ **Weston** ★★, one of the first Vermont villages to find fame in the

First B&B

There's a small inn or bed-and-breakfast around every bend in Vermont these days, but 40 years ago a cozy B&B was a real find. Such a place was the Markham House, in Weston. It was run by Asahel "Ace" Waite, a Yankee's Yankee, and his Sicilian wife, Katherine. Ace was in charge of breakfast—the secret of his fluffy scrambled eggs was cottage cheese—and Katherine was in charge of everything else that made the Markham House seem like home. When you got to know Ace, you got to know where there were native brook trout and what flies they were taking; even before you got to know Katherine, you were never in want of a kind word, a sweet smile, and something good to eat even if you were arriving late in the evening. Ace and Katherine helped set the standard for Vermont inn keeping, a standard that endures to this day.

61

Green Mountain Flyer

Animal sculptures, Brattleboro Museum & Art Center

outside world for its simple beauty. Opposite the serene town green, with its bandstand and iron fence, stands the **Weston Playhouse** *(802-824-5288 in season. Performances late June–Labor Day),* a summer stock tradition for over 60 years. Also near the green you'll find the 1790s **Farrar-Mansur House** *(Vt. 100. 802-824-4399. July-Aug. Wed.-Sun., fall weekends, and by appt.; donations),* a colonial tavern with seven original hearths. (Weston's first town meeting was held in the ballroom in 1800.) Among Weston's score of shops and galleries, the **Vermont Country Store** *(Vt. 100. 802-824-3184. Mon.-Sat.)* was founded a half century ago by local squire and writer Vrest Orton; it has grown into an emporium (and a huge mail-order business) filled with useful items ranging from woolen ware to kitchen equipment. At its heart, though, remains the potbellied stove. Next door, at the store's gastronomic equivalent, the **Bryant House Restaurant** *(Vt. 100. 802-824-6287. Mon.-Sat.)* serves Indian pudding and sandwiches of smoked ham and Vermont cheddar.

Four miles north of Weston, near the intersection of Vt. 100 and Vt. 155, lies the **Weston Priory** *(802-824-5409. Services most days),* a small Benedictine community. Sunday Masses feature liturgical music written by the brothers; a shop sells the priory's crafts, apples, and maple syrup.

Backtrack to Weston and from the green follow Andover Road east over the mountain. At Vt. 11, head farther east into **Chester,** notable for its broad main street and scattering of early 19th-century stone houses. Bear right just past Chester to follow Vt. 103 to US 5, and head south into **Bellows Falls.** Here you can catch the **Green Mountain Flyer** *(Green Mountain Railroad, 8 Depot Sq. 802-463-3069. Tues.-Sun. in summer; fall foliage and winter schedules vary; adm. fee)* for a scenic 26-mile ride to Chester and back in vintage coaches pulled by a diesel locomotive.

From Bellows Falls, take Vt. 121 west into the hills above the Connecticut River Valley to ❺ **Grafton**★ *(Information Center 802-843-2255. Mem. Day–Labor Day),* one of New England's most lovingly restored villages. A well-regarded hotel, the **Old Tavern at Grafton** *(Main St. and Townshend Rd. 802-843-2231 or 800-843-1801. Closed April)* sits in a comfortable nest of white clapboard buildings dating in part from 1788. The nearby **Grafton Historical Society Museum** *(Main St. 802-843-2584. Mem. Day-Columbus Day weekends only; adm. fee)* documents Grafton's transition from forgotten hill town to restored showplace. Grafton cheese, available in several shops around town, still rates among the best in a state known for its cheddar.

Leave Grafton via Vt. 121, backtracking as far as the attractive little prep school town of Saxtons River. Follow Westminster Street out of town and turn right on Westminster-West Road to **Putney.** Home of a small progressive school and a succession of colleges, Putney retains much of the countercultural atmosphere of a quarter century ago in its clutch of crafts shops and natural foods stores. The same spirit lingers in much larger ❻ **Brattleboro,** just down the road via US 5 south. The **Brattleboro Museum & Art Center** *(Lower Main St. 802-257-0124. May-Oct. Tues.-Sun.; adm. fee),* in a restored 1915 train station, focuses on contemporary art and local history. Stop for a look at native William Morris Hunt's 1851 painting "The Prodigal Son" at **Brooks Memorial Library** *(224 Main St. 802-254-5290. Mon.-Sat.).*

Sugarhouse in Putney

Travelers heading to northern Vermont or southern New England can pick up I-91 at Brattleboro. To complete the round-trip to Bennington, take Vt. 9—the **Molly Stark Trail.** Along the way, the well-paved "trail" passes by the music festival town of **Marlboro;** the village of **Wilmington,** with its cozy inns and access to ski resorts; and the southern reaches of the Green Mountain National Forest, ablaze with color in fall.

The Berkshires ★

120 miles ● 2 days ● Spring through fall ● Road to Mount Greylock is too narrow for RVs. Notch Road closed mid-October through mid-May.

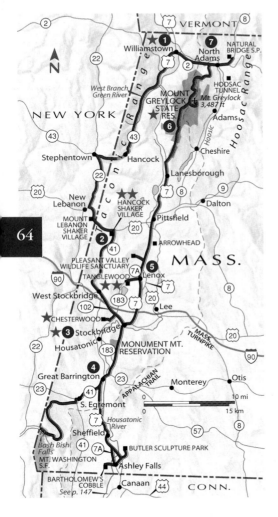

With a renown all out of proportion to their unprepossessing altitudes, western Massachusetts' Berkshire Hills have long been the retreat of rusticating city dwellers and a draw for culture lovers who come to enjoy art, music, and dance in the wooded surroundings. Lush back roads wind through a rolling landscape famous for its picture-perfect towns, literary legacies, and Gilded Age achievements in architecture and art collecting.

The route starts in the college town of Williamstown and meanders south, skirting (and briefly crossing) the New York state line to Great Barrington. Two side trips explore the rugged countryside before returning north through Norman Rockwell's beloved Stockbridge, climbing magnificent Mount Greylock, and visiting the old mill town of North Adams.

❶ Williamstown★ *(Board of Trade 413-458-9077)* is home of two celebrated art museums. The **Sterling and Francine Clark Art Institute★★** *(225 South St. 413-458-9545. Tues.-Sun.)* houses a superb collection of sculpture, silver, drawings, and prints from the 15th through the 19th centuries. But the museum is best known for its paintings by American masters and French Impressionists, including 34 Renoirs. Visitors often overlook the excellent **Williams College Museum of Art★** *(Lawrence Hall on Main St. 413-597-2429. Tues.-Sun.)*, strong in American art from the 18th through the 20th centuries.

The college's **Chapin Library of Rare Books★** *(2nd floor, Stetson Hall. 413-597-2462. Mon.-Fri.)* displays documents from the American Revolution, including George Washington's copy of *The Federalist* papers.

The route ambles south on US 7 and Mass. 43, along the West Branch Green River. Dipping into New York State, it pushes farther south on N.Y. 22 to US 20. You're now in Shaker country; two of the religious sect's 19 U.S. villages lie within a few miles of each other. The 25 buildings at the **Mount Lebanon Shaker Village** *(Darrow School, Shaker Rd., New Lebanon, N.Y. 518-794-9500. Daily July 4–Labor Day, weekends Mem. Day–July 4 and Labor Day–Columbus Day; adm. fee)* are all original, and the village looks much as it did in the 19th century. Back over the border in Massachusetts, each of the 20 buildings at the more elaborate, fully restored ❷ **Hancock Shaker Village** ★ ★ *(E on US 20. 413-443-0188. April-Nov.; adm. fee)* stand as a testament to the Shakers' ingenuity in design and craftsmanship. The epitome of efficacy, the three-story round barn, built of stone in 1826, enabled one farmer standing at its center to feed 52 cows at the same time.

65

Move south on Mass. 41 and Mass. 102 toward downtown ❸ **Stockbridge** ★ *(Berkshire Visitors Bureau 413-443-9186 or 800-237-5747)*. Trails at the **Berkshire Botanical Garden** *(Jct. of Mass. 102 and Mass. 183. 413-298-3926. May-Oct.; adm. fee)* lace 15 acres of perennial, herb, and vegetable beds.

South on Mass. 183, the works of one of America's favorite illustrators

Building facade at Hancock Shaker Village

chronicle the America everyone likes to remember at the **Norman Rockwell Museum at Stockbridge** ★ *(413-298-4100. Adm. fee)*. Between May and October you can also visit Rockwell's Stockbridge studio, moved here in 1986.

Down the road, look for Mohawk Lake Road and **Chesterwood** ★ *(413-298-3579. May-Oct.; adm. fee)*, the modest 1901 summer home and 1898 studio of Daniel

Hoosac Tunnel

The Hoosac Tunnel was one of the engineering triumphs—and laborers' tragedies—of 19th-century America. For 25 years workers burrowed beneath the Hoosac Range between the towns of Florida and North Adams, completing in 1875 the Boston and Maine Railroad's 25,000-foot tunnel. It cost about 20 million dollars and nearly 200 lives.

Chester French. In the high-ceilinged studio, the famed sculptor worked on his greatest work, the seated Lincoln for the Lincoln Memorial in Washington, D.C. Trails cross the lush grounds where French liked to stroll.

Backtrack to Mass. 102 and head east into Stockbridge proper. It's easy to understand why Rockwell lived in this protypical lovely New England town. Take a stroll along Main Street and stop by the **Red Lion Inn** *(413-298-5545),* established as a stagecoach stop in 1773. Even if you don't want a meal, go in and look around.

Stockbridge began in 1734 as a mission to the Housatonic Indians. An idealistic young missionary built the circa 1739 **Mission House** *(Main St. 413-298-3239. Mem. Day–Columbus Day; adm. fee)* for his bride. Moved to this site in 1928, it holds a fine collection of American decorative arts and furniture. The brick 1825 **Merwin House** *(14 Main St. 413-298-4703. June–mid-Oct. Tues., Thurs., Sat., and Sun.; adm. fee)* showcases a family's Victorian lifestyle with an eclectic assortment of European and American pieces.

Stanford White designed the 26-room, gabled-and-shingled **Naumkeag** ★ ★ *(Prospect Hill Rd. 413-298-3239. Mem. Day–Columbus Day; adm. fee)* for New York lawyer Joseph Hodges Choate. Completed in 1886, the "cottage" displays priceless antiques that include a 60-piece Oriental porcelain tea and coffee set. Landscape architect Fletcher Steele took 30 years to finish the stunning gardens.

Birdhouses for sale in Sheffield

Elegant public buildings donated by turn-of-the-century residents line the streets of ❹ **Great Barrington.** Built in 1858 of locally quarried blue dolomite, **St. James Episcopal Church** *(352 Main St. 413-528-1460)* possesses stunning stained-glass windows, particularly the "Wedding Feast."

Leave town on US 7, turn onto Mass. 23/41, and at South Egremont, watch for a small road to **Bash Bish Falls** *(Mount Washington S.F. 413-528-0330).* A short hike along a wooded stream brings you to the 200-foot cascade, which drops dramatically in a series of falls through a spectacular gorge.

Back on US 7, meander farther south to **Sheffield** and its many antique shops. At **Fellerman & Raabe Glassworks** *(534 S. Main St. 413-229-8533. Closed Mon. in winter)* visitors can watch artists create handblown glass pieces. Past the turnoff for Mass. 7A, follow Hewins Street and Shunpike Road to **Butler Sculpture Park** *(481 Shunpike Rd. 413-229-8924. May-Oct. or by appt.),* a woodlands sculpture garden set on a hilltop overlooking the Berkshires.

Remnants of marble and quartzite outcrops, or cobbles, formed under an inland sea more than 500 million years ago are found at **Bartholomew's Cobble** *(Weatogue Rd. 413-229-8600. Adm. fee),* west of Ashley Falls. Trails crisscross a variety of habitats whose soils nourish more than 800 species of vascular plants, including 53 different ferns. Just up Cooper Hill Road is the **Col. John Ashley House** *(413-298-3239. July–Labor Day Wed.-Sun. p.m., Mem. Day–Columbus Day weekends and holidays only; adm. fee),* a 1735 colonial dwelling with extensive herb gardens.

At Bartholomew's Cobble

67

Backtrack on US 7 through Great Barrington to **Monument Mountain Reservation** *(413-298-3239)* and hike up **Squaw Peak** for breathtaking views of the Berkshires. One rainy August day in 1850, authors Nathaniel Hawthorne and Herman Melville made the hike—the beginning of a lifelong friendship. The gentle Indian Monument Trail takes about an hour.

Continue north toward Lenox to the southern junction of US 7 and Mass. 7A, and **The Mount**★ *(2 Plunkett St. 413-637-1899. May-Oct.; adm. fee).* Designed by novelist Edith Wharton, the turn-of-the-century American classical style mansion, with its long halls and tall windows, reflects her love of balance and symmetry. Wharton created an Italian-style walled garden with proceeds from her successful novel, *The House of Mirth.*

In the resort town of ❺ **Lenox** *(Chamber of Commerce 413-637-3646),* head a mile out West Street (Mass. 183) to **Tanglewood**★★ *(413-637-1940 July-Aug., 617-638-9267 rest of year. Grounds open late June–early Sept.; fee for performances),* the 500-acre summer home of the Boston Symphony Orchestra. The Tanglewood Music Festival runs from late June through early September. Seating is available in a large shed or on the lawn. For the latter, bring a blanket and a picnic.

Inside The Mount, Edith Wharton's home in Lenox

Farther north, West Dugway Road leads to the Massachusetts Audubon Society's 1,500-acre **Pleasant Valley Wildlife Sanctuary** *(472 W. Mountain Rd. 413-637-0320. Sanctuary closed Mon. in winter; museum open May-Oct.; adm. fee).* Seven miles of trails traverse a variety of terrains, including beaver wetlands.

Just a few miles down the road, Herman Melville lived at **Arrowhead** *(780 Holmes Rd. 413-442-1793. Daily Mem. Day–Labor Day, Labor Day–Oct. Fri.-Mon.; adm. fee)* between 1850 and 1863. From his study in this partially restored 1780s farmstead, he could see the "purple prospect" of Mount Greylock, which reminded him of a great whale. Among the major works he wrote here was *Moby Dick.*

Incorporated in 1761, the small city of **Pittsfield** *(Berkshire Visitor's Bureau 413-443-9186 or 800-237-5747)* thrived as a 19th-century manufacturing center. Melville enthusiasts will want to visit the **Herman Melville Memorial Room** in the **Berkshire Athenaeum** *(1 Wendell Ave. 413-499-9486. Mon.-Sat.),* which maintains the world's largest collection of his personal memorabilia. The **Berkshire Museum★** *(39 South St. 413-443-7171. Daily July-Aug., closed Mon. rest of year; adm. fee),* dedicated to the arts and sciences, features paintings by such American masters as Albert Bierstadt and John Singleton Copley, a 2,300-year-old mummy, a 3,000-piece rock and mineral collection, and an aquarium-vivarium with more than 125 different species of fish and animals.

At **Lanesborough,** turn right onto North Main Street (later called Rockwell Road) for ❻ **Mount Greylock State Reservation★** *(413-499-4262),* encom-

passing the state's highest peak (3,487 feet). At the summit, an observation tower *(mid-May–mid-Oct.)* offers wonderful views of the Berkshire Valley and the Taconic Range. The rustic **Bascom Lodge** *(413-743-1591. Mid-May–mid-Oct.)* provides food and lodging.

Descend Mount Greylock via scenic Notch Road *(mid-May–mid-Oct.)*, then take Mass. 2 east a short way to ❼ **North Adams.** The mill town boomed after 1876, when the completion of the Hoosac Tunnel (see sidebar p. 66) made it an important waystop between Boston and points west. An exhibit at the **Western Gateway Heritage State Park** *(413-663-6312. Donations)* dramatically recounts the tunnel's story using sound and light.

A few miles north on Mass. 8, **Natural Bridge State Park** *(413-663-6392. Mem. Day–Columbus Day; adm. fee)*, site of an abandoned quarry, claims North America's only marble dam as well as a natural marble bridge. Return to Williamstown on a short stretch of the **Mohawk Trail,** a scenic 63-mile portion of Mass. 2 that traces an old Indian footpath.

Tower atop Mount Greylock

69

Berkshire sunrise from Mount Greylock

Pioneer Valley

165 miles ● 1 to 2 days ● Spring through late fall

Known as Pioneer Valley, this was the destination of America's first westward-bound pioneers—17th-century adventurers who, already feeling population pressures around Boston, left to find fertile land along the Connecticut River. The valley today holds not only reminders of these early settlers, but also of the great industries—textiles, tools, paper, and more—that grew here at the beginning of the 20th century. This is also Higher Education Valley, with the state's largest concentration of colleges after Boston.

The drive starts in Springfield, then roughly follows the Connecticut River Valley north to Northampton. Looping west to visit some of the pastoral hill towns of the Berkshires, the route rejoins the valley at Greenfield, then descends through the star-crossed pioneer settlement of Historic Deerfield, Emily Dickinson's Amherst, and industrial Holyoke before returning to Springfield.

Founded in 1636 by English fur trader William Pynchon, ❶ **Springfield** ★ *(Chamber of Commerce 413-787-1555)* is a patchwork of cultural and historic sites, faded industries, fine parks, and neighborhoods in all the shades and stages of the modern urban spectrum. An Italian Renaissance campanile marks **Court Square** *(Main and Court Sts.)*, the city's historical and governmental center. Springfield's major museums—art, science, and history—occupy three sides of the **Quadrangle** ★ ★ *(State and Chestnut Sts. 413-739-*

3871. Thurs.-Sun. p.m.; adm. fee), with the city library on the fourth. Next to the library, Augustus Saint-Gaudens' magnificent statue "The Puritan" memorializes early settler Deacon Samuel Chapin. The **Springfield Armory National Historic Site** ★ *(1 Armory Square. 413-734-8551. Tues.-Sun.)*, where the Army's 1903 Springfield rifles were manufactured, houses one of the world's most extensive

Statue at the Springfield Armory

firearms collections, dating from 1795 to 1968. Designed by the great 19th-century architect H.H. Richardson, **Hispanic Baptist Church** stands at the head of **Mattoon Street,** a gaslit block of brick row houses built in the 1870s.

In 1891 Springfield resident James Naismith thought up the game of throwing a soccer ball into a peach basket. Celebrate the result at the **Naismith Memorial Basketball Hall of Fame** ★ *(1150 W. Columbus Ave.*

Pioneer Valley

The Story of Dr. Seuss

Springfield can claim fame as the home of the Indian motorcycle, the M-1 rifle, and the game of basketball. But perhaps the most widely appreciated of all Springfield's gifts to the world was a native son named Theodor Seuss Geisel, better known as Dr. Seuss.

Theodor Geisel was born in 1904, the son of the park department superintendent who oversaw Springfield's Forest Park Zoo. As a boy Theodor spent long hours at the zoo at one of his favorite pastimes, sketching the animals. As far as we know, none of those creatures had more than the usual number of joints or appendages. . . but we know very well how they evolved in the artist's imagination.

There's still a zoo in Forest Park, a spacious retreat on the south side of the city. And little Ted Geisel? He became rich and famous with a book about a cat.

413-781-6500. Adm. fee). When you weary of three levels of basketball history, including replicas of the original peach baskets and balls, shoot some hoops yourself at the Spalding Shootout.

Nearly 200 animals reside at the **Zoo in Forest Park** (Mass. 83 off Sumner Ave. 413-733-2251. Daily mid-April–mid-Nov., weekends rest of year; adm. fee), successor to the old zoo once supervised by the father of Theodor Geisel, also known as Dr. Seuss. The huge park (entry fee for cars) also offers playing fields, pedal boats, and rambling paths.

Follow signs for the "Big E"—the Eastern States Exposition, held each September—into West Springfield and **Storrowton Village Museum** (1305 Memorial Ave. 413-787-0136. Mid-June–Labor Day Mon.-Sat., rest of year by appt.; adm. fee). Seven 18th- and 19th-century buildings moved here from throughout New England give visitors a fair—if somewhat glamorized—sense of what life was like in an early American village.

West on US 20 is ❷ **Westfield,** where you'll find **Stanley Park** (400 Western Ave. 413-568-9312), a 300-acre jewel in the Berkshire foothills. From May through September the park's award-winning rose, annual, and perennial gardens put on a showy display. The 160-acre **Frank Stanley Beveridge Memorial Wildlife Sanctuary,** on park grounds, abuts the shores of the Little River.

The route weaves north on Mass. 10 toward Northampton. For a bird's-eye view of where the Connecticut River loops to form an oxbow, detour 5 miles east to **Mount Tom State Reservation** (413-527-4805). A progressively rougher road leads to Goat Peak, near the top of 1,214-foot Mount Tom. Climb the tower or hike around Lake Bray for magnificent views of the valley below.

Continuing north on Mass. 10, watch for a small sign marking the road to the Massachusetts Audubon Society's **Arcadia Nature Center and Wildlife Sanctuary** (127 Combs Rd., Easthampton. 413-584-3009. Tues.-Sun.; adm. fee). Among the 600 acres of marshlands, fields, and woods are several ecologically unusual areas of floodplain forest.

The town of ❸ **Northampton**★ (Chamber of Commerce 413-584-1900) owes much of its vibrancy to **Smith College** (Main Street. 413-584-2700), founded in 1871 "to develop as fully as may be the powers of womanhood." Its **Museum of Art**★★ (Elm St. at Bedford Terrace. 413-585-2760. Tues.-Sun.) has one of the country's finest college collections of 19th- and 20th-century French and American paintings. Horticulture and botany are taught at the **Lyman Plant House**★ *(College Lane. 413-585-2748),* which also provides an oasis on gray days for students and visitors alike. Plants and flowers thrive in a variety of simulated climates, including tropical flora in the Palm House.

The **Calvin Coolidge Memorial Room** in the Forbes Library *(20 West St. 413-584-6037. Mon.-Wed.)* honors the city's former mayor and state governor (and later U.S. President) with Coolidge memorabilia. A comprehensive collection of original art at the **Words & Pictures Museum** *(140 Main St. 413-586-8545. Tues.-Sun.; adm. fee)* pays homage to "sequential art"—comic books. The second floor Interactive Zone offers imaginative visitors a chance to put their own comic strips together.

The **Northampton Historical Society** *(46 Bridge St. 413-584-6011. March-Dec. Wed.-Sun. p.m.)* maintains three period houses in various stages of restoration: the circa 1730 **Parsons House,** the circa 1796 **Pomeroy-Shepherd House,** and the **Isaac Damon House** (circa 1813).

West on Mass. 9 lies the attractive village of **Williamsburg.** The **Williamsburg General Store** *(12 Main St. 413-268-3036)* opened its doors in 1874 to provide locals with daily necessities. Today it sells a hodgepodge of homemade baked goods, jams, jellies, crafts, and ice cream. A sign on the door sends you "just 174 steps" (strides, actually) to the beautifully restored **Williams House** *(4 Main St. 413-268-7300),* which has served meals to the public since 1813. Near the house, look for Petticoat Hill Road, leading to the trailhead for 1,185-foot **Petticoat Hill** *(413-298-3239).* At the top you'll be treated to some great valley views. Back in town, **Williamsburg Blacksmiths** *(Goshen Rd. 413-268-7341. Mon.-Sat.)* makes reproductions of early American wrought-iron hardware in a reproduced 1840s mill.

Leaving town, drive west on Mass. 143 and start the climb to the hill town of ❹ **Chesterfield,** renowned for its

Main Street, Northampton

maple syrup. During the March-April season, the Massachusetts Maple Phone *(413-628-3912)* gives regular recorded boiling updates and a list of sugarhouses. The Department of Environmental Management offers an informative look at the sugaring process at **Krug Sugarbush** *(South St., East Branch/D.A.R. State Forest. 413-268-7098. March-April).*

Cross over the Westfield River and follow signs to rugged **Chesterfield Gorge**★ *(River Rd. W. 413-298-3239).* Over millions of years, glacial ice and the rushing waters of the Westfield River carved the deep canyon between sheer granite cliffs. A hiking trail wends along the bluff above the gorge. At the upper end of the narrows rest the remains of the High Bridge, built in 1739, and a small settlement that grew up around the gatekeeper's house.

Continue west on Mass. 143 to Mass. 112 and turn north toward **Cummington.** William Cullen Bryant, the poet and owner-editor of the *New York Evening Post,* grew up at the ❺ **William Cullen Bryant Homestead**★ *(Bryant Rd. 413-634-2244. Late June–Labor Day Fri.-Sun. p.m., Labor Day–mid-Oct. Sat.-Sun.; adm. fee),* a 21-room clapboard mansion overlooking the Hampshire hills and the Westfield River Valley. In 1865, at age 71, he bought it back as his summer residence. The cottage-style bedroom furniture was among the nation's first to be mass produced.

Farm outside Ashfield

Farther north, near the high, wooded town of **Ashfield,** the Trustees of Reservations *(413-298-3239)* owns two very different properties, each with scenic hiking trails: **Bear Swamp Reservation** *(Hawley Rd.)* is an undeveloped tract of beaver ponds and streams; while **Chapelbrook Reservation** *(Williamsburg Rd., 3.8 miles south of Town Hall)* contains three levels of waterfalls.

Six miles east on Mass. 116 lies the picturesque hill

town of **Conway,** once the home of poet Archibald MacLeish. Native son and Chicago department store founder Marshall Field donated the handsome **Field Memorial Library** on the triangular town green.

Just beyond Conway, turn left and follow Shelburne Falls Road to ❻ **Shelburne Falls,** straddling the Deerfield River. As a living memorial to the war heroes of Shelburne and nearby Buckland, the local garden club planted flowers on an old trolley bridge, in bloom from early spring through late fall. Just downstream look for the **Salmon Falls Glacial Potholes,** circular holes ground out of granite during the Ice Ages.

Border collie demonstration at the Ashfield Fall Festival

For 9 miles the route follows the **Mohawk Trail,** a 63-mile scenic stretch of Mass. 2 named after a footpath blazed by Mohawk Indians. At Greenfield, take Mass. 2A east to US 5, which zips south to ❼ **Historic Deerfield** ★ ★ *(413-774-5581. Adm. fee).* The place has been described as a beautiful ghost, inhabited by the spirits of those who witnessed life in this small New England town over 300 years ago, including ferocious, French-instigated Indian attacks. If there *are* ghosts here, there's lots of room for them. Fifty-two 18th- and 19th-century buildings stretch for a mile along Old Deerfield's main street—called The Street. Fourteen are open to the public by guided tour on an alternating schedule. Among the highlights: the **Henry Needham Flynt Silver and Metalware Collection,** with more than 1,500 pieces of American and English silver, and the **Helen Geier Flynt Textile Museum,** housed in an 1872 barn and exhibiting early textiles, needlework, and costumes. The **Channing Blake Meadow Walk** encompasses agricultural and natural landscapes and offers views of the Pocumtuck Ridge and Shelburne Hills.

As a contrast, the eclectic collection of antiques and artifacts at the **Memorial Hall Museum** ★ *(8 Memorial St. 413-774-3768. May-Oct.; adm. fee)* includes ornate Hadley chests and posters promoting Mack, the 4,700-pound ox. For a lovely spot to rest and dine between house tours try the **Deerfield Inn** *(81 Old Main St. 413-774-5587).*

Pioneer Valley

Overlooking Sunderland and the Connecticut River from Sugarloaf Mountain

Continue south on US 5 to South Deerfield and the **Yankee Candle Car Museum** *(413-665-2020. Adm. fee),* which lives up to its motto, "cars that make you go wow," with more than 75 exotic cars from Europe and the United States. Across the street, check out the museum at the popular **Yankee Candle Company**★ *(413-665-8306),* and be sure to see the fabulous Bavarian Christmas Village. Save time to hand-dip a few candles.

Southeast of town, at the 532-acre **Mount Sugarloaf State Reservation** *(South Deerfield. 413-625-2939),* take in the fine view of the Pioneer Valley and Connecticut River.

❽ Amherst★ *(Chamber of Commerce 413-253-0700)* possesses the cosmopolitan air you'd expect of a town with three major colleges and universities, but it still retains much of the quiet atmosphere enjoyed by lifelong resident Emily Dickinson. The reclusive poet spent virtually her entire life (1830-1886) inside the federal **Dickinson Homestead**★ *(280 Main St. 413-542-8161. May-Oct. Wed.-Sat. p.m., early spring and late fall Wed. and Sat. p.m. Appt. advised; adm. fee).* Harvard University now holds the bulk of her personal belongings, but you'll find her re-created bedroom study here. Tour guides reveal interesting details about her life and works.

Many of Dickinson's original manuscripts, letters, and memorabilia are housed in the Special Collections Department of the **Jones Library** *(43 Amity St. 413-256-4090. Mon.-Sat. during academic year; call for summer hours).* Here too are the manuscripts and letters of poet Robert Frost, another one-time Amherst resident.

Decorative arts, paintings, tools, and period rooms in the **Amherst History Museum at the Strong House** *(67 Amity St. 413-256-0678. Mid-May–mid-Oct. Wed.-Sat. p.m., winter by appt.; adm. fee)* give visitors a feel for everyday life in Amherst over the last 300 years.

On the Amherst College campus consider visiting two intriguing museums. Not all the exhibits at the **Pratt Museum of Natural History**★ *(413-542-2165. Closed weekdays in summer)* are as dramatic as its mastodon skeleton, but they give laypeople an understanding of vertebrate evolution. The **Mead Art Museum**★ *(413-542-2335. Closed Mon. June-Aug.)* is a wonderful place to introduce children to art. It's small enough not to be overwhelming, yet holds a superb collection of American and European paintings. In one wing, a 1611 English Jacobean-Renaissance room has been installed in its entirety.

Continue south on Mass. 116 to **South Hadley** and **Mount Holyoke College** *(413-538-2000)*, founded in 1837 as one of the country's first women's colleges. The firm of Frederick Law Olmsted, creator of New York's Central Park, landscaped the grounds. Founded in 1876, the **Mount Holyoke College Art Museum**★ *(413-538-2245. Tues.-Sun.)* is one of the oldest art museums in the nation and houses more than 13,000 works, ranging from ancient Egyptian to contemporary paintings and sculpture. Three buildings at the **Joseph Allen Skinner Museum** *(35 Woodbridge St. 413-538-2085. May-Oct. Wed. and Sun. p.m.)* display an eclectic combination of farm implements, decorative glass, Indian artifacts, medieval armor, and mounted birds.

Farther south on Mass. 116, ❾ **Holyoke** *(Chamber of Commerce 413-534-3376)* calls itself the first planned industrial city in the country (there are other contenders). Though its days as a major paper manufacturer are long gone, the canals and redbrick mills still stand. The **Wistariahurst Museum** *(238 Cabot St. 413-534-2216. Wed., Sat., and Sun. p.m.; adm. fee)*, a beaux-arts mansion with vaulted ceilings, grand oak staircase, and elegant furnishings provides a glimpse into the opulent lifestyle of a silk manufacturer.

There's plenty to do downtown at **Holyoke Heritage State Park** *(Between Dwight and Appleton Sts.)*. A well-executed audiovisual exhibit in the **Visitor Center** *(221 Appleton St. 413-534-1723)* overviews the city's industrial history. Fun, hands-on activities pack the **Children's Museum** *(444 Dwight St. 413-536-KIDS. Tues.-Sun.; adm. fee)*. In the same building, the small **Volleyball Hall of Fame** *(413-536-0926. Tues.-Sun.)* pays tribute to the game born in Holyoke. Finally, hop on a hand-carved horse at one of the country's few remaining grand carousels *(June–Labor Day Tues.-Sun., weekends rest of year; fare)*.

Johnson Chapel on the Amherst College Green

Blackstone-Quabbin Route ★

135 miles ● 2 to 3 days ● Late spring through mid-autumn ● Old Sturbridge Village can easily take the best part of a day.

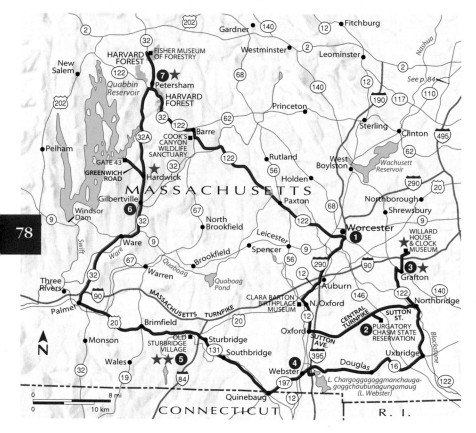

Sometimes overlooked by travelers winging along the Massachusetts Turnpike between Boston and the Berkshires, this central swath of the Bay State offers considerable variety in both scenery and historical associations. The drive takes in Worcester, New England's second largest city, and ranges along the once heavily industrialized, but now tranquil, Blackstone River Valley. It then heads back into preindustrial New England by way of deliberately preserved Old Sturbridge Village and the accidentally preserved hill towns along the lonely stretches of blacktop east of the Quabbin Reservoir.

The drive begins in Worcester, then swings south and east to include sites connected with American pioneers in nursing and clockmaking, with a look at a bizarre topographical feature. Stop to stroll along an old canal, then take a swim in the lake with the longest name of any body of water in America. After visiting the past at Sturbridge, drive north into near-wilderness, where such timeless villages as Hardwick and Petersham seem to have been transported from northern New Hampshire or Vermont.

1 **Worcester** *(Chamber of Commerce 508-753-2924)* belies its aging factory-town image with the diversity of its educational environment (there are 10 colleges in the city and the surrounding area) and the variety of its museums and cultural institutions. While concert-goers praise the acoustics at venerable **Mechanics Hall** *(321 Main St. 508-752-5608)* and scholars mine centuries of archives at the **American Antiquarian Society** *(185 Salisbury St. 508-755-5221. Mon.-Fri.)*, art lovers enjoy central Massachusetts' most comprehensive collection at the **Worcester Art Museum** ★ *(55 Salisbury St. 508-799-4406. Wed.-Sun.; adm. fee)*. The museum's holdings fill 48 galleries, ranging from preclassical sculpture to 19th-century French Impressionism to 20th-century paintings, photographs, prints, and decorative arts. The **Higgins Armory Museum** ★ *(100 Barber Ave. 508-853-6015. Tues.-Sun.; adm. fee)* has a far more pointed collecting philosophy. Founded by steel magnate John Woodman Higgins, this treasury of medieval and Renaissance armor and weaponry is housed in a suitably castlelike interior where kids can even try on pieces of the steel suits.

On the city's outskirts, the **New England Science Center** *(222 Harrington Way. 508-791-9211. Adm. fee)* combines a planetarium, aquarium, and environmental exhibits with a train ride through 60 acres of woodlands.

Grafton Common

Leave Worcester via I-290 and take Mass. 12 south to **North Oxford**. The **Clara Barton Birthplace Museum** *(66 Clara Barton Rd. 508-987-5375. April-Oct.; adm. fee)*, the modest circa 1820 home of the American Red Cross

Father of Rocketry

Worcester native Robert Goddard (1882-1945) was the father of modern rocketry. A physics professor at Clark University, the rocket scientist launched the first successful liquid-fuel rocket from a site near the city in 1926. An exhibit of early rocket hardware, photographs, murals, and interpretive displays on Clark's Worcester campus in the **Goddard Library** *(950 Main St. 508-793-7461)* documents his achievements.

founder, contains family furnishings, early 19th-century kitchen and household equipment, Civil War artifacts (Barton volunteered as a nurse on the front lines), and memorabilia from the early Red Cross days.

Four miles south in **Oxford,** notable for its broad main street and proud Greek Revival houses, turn left on Sutton Avenue (later Central Turnpike). Then head east 7 miles to Purgatory Road and ❷ **Purgatory Chasm State Reservation** *(508-234-3733. Trail closed in winter; not advisable when wet)*. Considered a geological curiosity as early as 1793, the mad jumble of enormous boulders clutters a cleft in the native granite that in some places reaches 70 feet in depth. The trail from the parking area doesn't lead *to* the chasm, but *through* it. Anyone attempting the half-mile round-trip should be in good shape and wear sturdy shoes.

Return to Central Turnpike and continue east to Northbridge, then north on Mass. 122 to ❸ **Grafton**★, a village so quintessentially New England that the movie version of Eugene O'Neill's *Ah, Wilderness!* was filmed on and around its unusual oval common. Head out of town via North Street and follow signs for the **Willard House and Clock Museum**★ *(11 Willard St. 508-839-3500. Tues.-Sun.; adm. fee)*. The oldest part of this rambling house dates from 1718, but its interest derives from the four clock-making Willard brothers who lived and worked here during the late 18th century. Willard clocks—particularly those made by Simon Willard—were the ne plus ultra of timekeeping in their day, and are still prized by collectors. Dozens upon dozens of Willard clocks tick away within these walls; the guided tour takes in several rooms of family furnishings and an authentic 18th-century clockmaker's workshop.

Willard House and Clock Museum, Grafton

Ten miles south, **Uxbridge** is one of the keystone towns of the **Blackstone River Valley National Heritage Corridor** *(508-278-7604)*. Flowing 46 miles from Worcester to Providence, Rhode Island, the Blackstone River provided water power for some of New England's earliest

Blackstone River from King Philip's Rock in Northbridge

manufacturing experiments. By the mid-19th century, the Blackstone was the nation's most heavily industrialized river valley. The region's industrial prowess has long since faded, but important touchstones survive.

Nearly all traces of busy little Uxbridge fade away as you walk along the towpath of the old **Blackstone Canal** *(Mendon Rd.),* opened in 1828 to allow barge traffic to move from the hinterlands to the sea. To the west of the towpath is a pocket wilderness of marshes, woods, and meadows. The **River Bend Farm Visitor Center** *(287 Oak St. 508-278-7604)* occupies a restored dairy barn a mile north. Continue a short distance to the stone arch bridge, which casts a lovely reflection on the canal.

Ambling west, the drive comes to Lake Webster, whose original Algonquian name would make a Welshman stutter with envy: **Chargoggagoggmanchaugagoggchaubunagungamaug** simply means "You fish on your side, I'll fish on my side, and no one fishes in the middle." At **Memorial Beach** *(Memorial Beach Dr. Summer; parking fee)* in the town of ❹ **Webster,** a walk or swim along a scenic, protected cove offers fine views of the lake's forested shores.

Farther west in Sturbridge, ❺ **Old Sturbridge Village**★★ *(1 Old Sturbridge Village Rd. 508-347-3362. April-Oct., call for winter schedule; adm. fee)* faithfully represents, in spirit and character, a thousand New England villages as they appeared between the American Revolution and the transitional years of the 1830s. Collected from all around New England and moved to this 200-acre site, some 40 of that era's buildings (and some built on the

Interpretive guide at Old Sturbridge Village

82

site) make up the village. Early furnishings, tools, housewares, and trade goods fill the structures, and costumed interpreters describe their long-ago counterparts' lives. A printer prints in the printing office; cobblers make shoes; and a minister welcomes visitors to his parsonage. Throughout the year, guides present demonstrations of the crafts and activities of two centuries ago; water-powered milling of grain and wood, bread baking, and black-powder musket firing are but a few. The menu at the tavern-style restaurant runs to cornbread and pot pies. Ranking with such places as Colonial Williamsburg and Plimoth Plantation, Old Sturbridge Village is one of the nation's premier living history establishments.

Leaving Sturbridge, pick up US 20 and head west through **Brimfield,** which hosts mammoth outdoor antique shows in the fields just west of town each May, July, and September. Turn north at Palmer onto Mass. 32, and continue past the old brick buildings of Ware to ❻ **Gilbertville.** A part of Hardwick (thus the name on the town hall), the village boasts a handsome granite church and a little beaux-arts library. The most distinctive structure in town is the 1886 **covered bridge** *(Left off Mass. 32),* across the Ware River. Unlike most New England covered bridges, this one can accommodate two cars, or horse-drawn carriages, at once.

Bear left onto Mass. 32A where it diverges from Mass. 32 and travel a few miles north to **Hardwick ★,** a federal and Greek Revival period piece of a village clustered around a classic upcountry common. The Civil War monument looks south, as the best ones do up this way, and the chaste church facades of New England's old theological adversaries, the Congregationalists and the Unitarians, face each other across the common.

At Hardwick Common's southern end, turn left onto Greenwich Road for a short drive to Gate 43 of the **Quabbin Reservoir** *(413-323-7221. Pedestrian access only through numbered gates. Call for information on fishing and other permitted activities).* The source of fresh water for almost half the state, Quabbin was created in the 1930s by the damming of the Swift River. Covering 39 square miles and containing upward of 400 billion gallons of water when full, it completely covered four entire towns whose residents—living and dead—were either bought out or moved to new locations by the state. This vast central portion of the state has reverted to the status of a little-known semi-wilderness.

One of the loneliest and most scenic drives in the state, the 10-mile stretch from Hardwick to Petersham offers occasional views of the reservoir and its valley to the west, when the trees aren't in leaf. Just beyond the point where Mass. 32A rejoins Mass. 32 lies **❼ Petersham★** *(Chamber of Commerce 978-368-7687)*, a typical hill town built along a ridge with fine views toward the east. Along its common, the Greek Revival houses, church, and town hall, with its gilded cupola, represent the best of early 19th-century rural New England architecture.

Petersham has a tidy country store with a small restaurant and ice-cream parlor. Just north of town, the **Petersham Craft Center** *(Mass. 32. 978-724-3415. April-Dec. Tues.-Sun.)* sells jewelry, ceramics, and other works by local artisans. Set at the edge of a 3,000-acre preserve that acts as a "teaching forest" for forestry students at Harvard University, the **Fisher Museum of Forestry** *(Mass. 32. 978-724-3302. Closed weekends Nov.–April; donations)* features remarkable 3-dimensional dioramas that explain the evolution of New England's forests and man's interaction with them. Be sure to take a close look at the dioramas' trees, exquisitely realistic creations of copper wire, well worth a stop for their craftsmanship alone.

Overlooking the Quabbin Reservoir

Just outside Barre, the Massachusetts Audubon Society maintains the **Cook's Canyon Wildlife Sanctuary** *(South St. 781-259-9500. Adm. fee)*. Here, stretch your legs along a half-mile trail following the course of Galloway Brook and its wooded canyon, which really falls into the smaller category of a ravine.

Boston and Beyond ★★

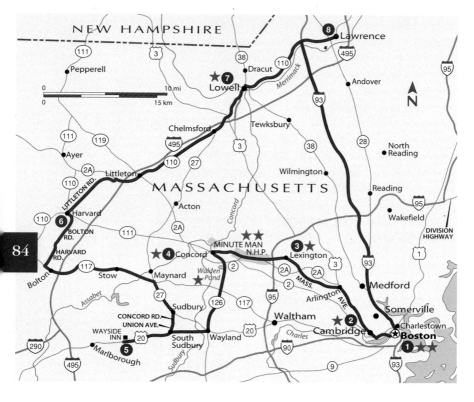

This drive in eastern Massachusetts links the birthplaces of two American revolutions—the American Revolution itself, which gained intellectual force in Boston and flashed into life when the muskets fired on Lexington Green, and the American industrial revolution, which began when capital and labor were added to the force of the Merrimack River at Lowell and Lawrence. Along the way is Concord, where the American literary renaissance flowered more than a century ago.

The route begins in Boston, crosses the Charles River to Cambridge, then sets out, like Paul Revere, for Lexington and Concord. After circling west through the manicured countryside of Boston's western suburbs, the drive takes in the former textile cities of Lowell and Lawrence.

Most of ❶ **Boston's** ★★ (*Greater Boston Convention & Visitors Bureau 617-536-4100 or 800-888-5515*) principal attractions are tucked onto the small peninsula where, in 1630, the Puritans founded their "city on a hill." The Revolutionary era comes to life along the **Freedom Trail**★★, a 2.5-mile walking route that connects 16 landmarks related to American independence. It begins downtown at **Boston Common,** the nation's oldest public park, wanders through the historic North End, and ends up across the Charles River at the Charlestown Navy Yard. *(For information on schedules and fees for sites listed below, call or visit the Boston National Historical Park Visitor Center, 15 State St. 617-242-5642. Or stop by the Visitor Information Center on Boston Common, Tremont and Park Sts.)*

Along the way you'll visit the Bulfinch-designed **Massachusetts State House** *(Beacon St.),* the state government seat for 200 years; **Park Street Church** *(Park and Tremont Sts.),* where abolitionist William Lloyd Garrison made his first Boston speech in 1829; and the **Old Granary Burying Ground** *(Tremont St.),* the resting place of Paul Revere, Samuel Adams, and other patriots. Sam Adams launched the Boston Tea Party at the **Old South Meeting House** *(310 Washington St.),* while the 1713 **Old State House** *(State St.)* was the colonial capitol. **Faneuil Hall** *(Merchants Row),* a popular gathering place for colonial dissidents, became known as the Cradle of Liberty.

The trail continues in Boston's North End, where the circa 1680 **Paul Revere House** *(19 North Sq.)* is the oldest building in downtown Boston. Nearby, signal lanterns that hung at the **Old North Church** *(193 Salem St.)* warned citizens of British troop movements on the eve of the battles of Lexington and Concord.

Across the Charles River in Charlestown, the Battle of Bunker Hill is re-created in a multimedia diorama at the **Bunker Hill Pavilion** *(55 Constitution Rd.).* Just uphill, visitors can climb the 220-foot granite **Bunker Hill Monument.** The trail ends at the Charlestown Navy Yard, berth of the nearly 200-year-old **U.S.S. *Constitution*.** A museum explains the ship's undefeated career and how it earned the name Old Ironsides.

85

Old State House in the heart of downtown Boston

Parading through Boston's historic North End

Not all of Boston's important attractions are on the Freedom Trail. The **New England Aquarium**★★ *(Central Wharf. 617-973-5200. Adm. fee)* features a four-story saltwater tank alive with tropical fish from the Atlantic Ocean. An original tea chest is one of many exhibits at the **Boston Tea Party Ship and Museum** *(Congress St. Bridge. 617-338-1773. Mar.-Nov.; adm. fee)*, housed in a replica of one of the infamous tea party ships. At the fun-filled **Children's Museum**★ *(300 Congress St. 617-426-8855. Tues.-Sun.; adm. fee)*, kids can walk on a giant's desk (where pencils and erasers are 12 times their normal size) and explore a two-story Japanese house. Next door, the **Computer Museum**★ *(300 Congress St. 617-426-2800. Tues.-Sun.; adm. fee)* lets visitors experiment with the latest uses of computer technology; exhibits also document computer history from the vacuum-tube era to the present.

The narrow, gaslit streets of **Beacon Hill** *(Beacon St. between Cambridge St. and the Charles River. Walking tour info 617-742-1854)* are worth a few hours' stroll for their early 19th-century architecture and abundant historical associations. Two worthwhile stops: the **African Meeting House** *(8 Smith Ct., off Joy St. 617-742-1854. Daily Mem. Day–Labor Day, Mon.-Fri. rest of year; donations)*, a restored 1806 church in which the New England Antislavery Society was founded in 1832, and the **Harrison Gray Otis House**★ *(141 Cambridge St. 617-227-3956. Tues.-Sat.; adm. fee)*, which offers a glimpse of genteel Boston society in the years after the Revolution.

Boston's preeminent art museums are the **Museum of Fine Arts**★★ *(465 Huntington Ave. 617-267-9300. Tues.-Sun.; adm. fee)*, world famous for its French Impressionist paintings, Asiatic collections, and American paintings and decorative arts, and the **Isabella Stewart Gardner Museum**★★ *(280 The Fenway. 617-566-1401. Tues.-Sun.; adm. fee)*, a replica of a Venetian palazzo built in 1899 by Mrs. Gardner to house her esteemed art collection. Since her death in 1924, nothing has been added or sold from her original holdings, which are strongest in Italian Renaissance art but span 30 centuries. Try to arrange your visit to coincide with one of the delightful concerts, held in the Tapestry Room.

About 3 miles south of downtown, the **John F. Kennedy Library and Museum**★ *(Columbia Point. 617-929-4523. Adm. fee)* offers an in-depth look at the life and legacy of the President whom Bostonians claim as their own. On the other side of town, hundreds of participatory exhibits at the **Museum of Science**★★ *(Science Park. 617-723-2500. Adm. fee)* explain everything from basic principles to applied technology.

Leaving Boston, drive across the Charles River to ❷ **Cambridge**★ *(Office for Tourism 617-441-2884 or 800-862-5678. Visitor Information booth at Harvard Sq. subway stop)*, one of the world's great educational centers. At Harvard Square, walk through the iron gates into Harvard Yard, the heart of 360-year-old **Harvard University**★★ *(Visitor information 617-495-1573)*. Harvard has three art museums *(617-495-9400. Tues.-Sun.; one adm. fee for all)*: the **Fogg**★ *(32 Quincy St.)*, featuring American and European collections; the **Busch-Reisinger**★ *(Werner Otto Hall; enter through Fogg)*, specializing in northern European art, particularly German expressionism; and the **Arthur M. Sackler**★ *(485 Broadway)*, concentrating on classical, Asian, and Islamic art. The university's **Museums of Cultural and Natural History** *(26 Oxford St. 617-495-3045. Adm. fee)* encompass the **Botanical Museum,** with its collection of 3,000 exquisitely detailed glass flowers; the **Mineralogical and Geological Museum;** the **Museum of Comparative Zoology;** and the **Peabody Museum of Archaeology and Ethnology.**

Statue of John Harvard, Harvard Yard, Cambridge

From Harvard Square drive west on Brattle Street to the **Longfellow National Historic Site** *(105 Brattle St. 617-876-4491. May-Oct. Wed.-Sun.; adm. fee)*, the 1759 Georgian mansion where Henry Wadsworth Longfellow resided for over 40 years. Here you can see many of the poet's books and furnishings.

Return to Harvard Square and take Massachusetts Avenue 10 miles west to ❸ **Lexington**★ *(Greater Merrimack Valley Convention & Visitors Bureau 978-459-6150 or 800-443-3332)*. On a cool morning in April 1775 Minute Men and British soldiers exchanged the first shots of the Ameri-

Boston and Beyond

can Revolution at **Lexington Green ★**. Several sites around the green recall the events leading up to that day. For orientation, stop by the **Lexington Visitor Center** *(1875 Massachusetts Ave. 781-862-1450)*, where a detailed diorama explains the battle. Nearby are the 1709 **Buckman Tavern** *(1 Bedford St. 781-862-5598. Mid-April–Oct.; adm. fee)*, furnished as it was when the Minute Men gathered here before the battle; and the **Hancock-Clarke House** *(36 Hancock St. 781-861-0928. Mid-April–Oct.; adm. fee)*, where Paul Revere and William Dawes warned Samuel Adams and John Hancock of the impending attack.

Just outside downtown Lexington, the British used **Munroe Tavern** *(1332 Massachusetts Ave. 781-862-1703. Mid-April–Oct.; adm. fee)* as a field headquarters and hospital after the Battle of Concord. It looks as it did then, right down to a bullet hole in the ceiling.

Around the corner at the **Museum of Our National Heritage** *(33 Marrett Rd. 781-861-6559)*, the Scottish Rite Masonic order offers changing exhibits and an extensive library of American history and society.

Proceed west on Massachusetts Avenue or Mass. 2A to **Minute Man National Historical Park ★ ★** *(978-369-6993)*, which straddles much of the Battle Road between Lexington and Concord. A film and displays at the **Battle Road Visitor Center** *(Mass. 2A. 781-862-7753. Mid-April–Oct.)* explain troop movements. Nearby, part of the Battle Road is preserved as a footpath.

Commemorating the Battle of Lexington, Lexington Green

Several miles west in ❹ **Concord ★**, another unit of the park centers around a replica of the **North Bridge ★**, marking the spot where the "shot heard round the world" was fired on April 19, 1775. Daniel Chester French's famous statue of the Minute Man with his plow and musket stands nearby, and a film, diorama, and colonial-era military paraphernalia at the **North Bridge Visitor Center** *(174 Liberty St. 978-369-6993)* detail battle events.

Concord's fame spills into the literary realm, for it was here that the American literary renaissance flourished a century and a half ago. In 1834-35 essayist and poet Ralph Waldo Emerson resided at the **Old Manse** *(269 Monument St. 978-369-3909. Mid-April–Oct. Wed.-Mon.)* while writing his seminal essay *Nature*. Later, Nathaniel

Hawthorne rented the colonial house and wrote *Mosses from an Old Manse.* Emerson and Hawthorne memorabilia are on display.

Hawthorne also lived at **The Wayside** *(455 Lexington Rd. 978-369-6975. Mid-Apr.–Oct. Thurs.-Tues.; adm. fee),* a part of the historical park. Later famous residents were the

North Bridge in Concord

Alcott family, including the transcendentalist philosopher A. Bronson Alcott and his daughter, author Louisa May Alcott. The Alcotts lived for a much longer time at the nearby **Orchard House** *(399 Lexington Rd. 978-369-4118. Closed first two weeks in Jan.; adm. fee),* a rambling, possibly pre-1700 structure that's almost entirely furnished with Alcott furniture and possessions. Louisa May wrote *Little Women* here. Especially endearing are the bedroom wall drawings by her sister May Alcott, who became an accomplished artist.

Ralph Waldo Emerson, the Sage of Concord, lived for nearly 50 years in the **Emerson House** *(28 Cambridge Tpk. 978-369-2236. Mid-Apr.–Oct. Thurs.-Sun.; adm. fee),* which has been preserved with almost all its furnishings. His study was moved intact across the street to the **Concord Museum★** *(200 Lexington Rd. 978-369-9609. Adm. fee).* Devoted to the town's history from Indian times through the 20th century, the museum's splendidly furnished period rooms document three centuries of tastes and occupations. Rounding out the collection are costumes, old silver, weapons used during the Battle of Concord, and a fascinating room filled with the possessions of a man who thought little of possessions—Concord's own Henry David Thoreau.

Thoreau himself is at rest on Author's Ridge in **Sleepy Hollow Cemetery** *(Mass. 62),* just outside busy Concord center. Here too are the graves of Emerson, Hawthorne, the Alcotts, and the sculptor Daniel Chester French.

The drive heads south out of town to a place forever associated with Thoreau, **Walden Pond★** *(Walden Pond*

State Reservation. Mass. 126. 978-369-3254. No pets. Park closes when parking lot reaches capacity. Parking fee in summer). The half-mile-long pond and its surrounding woods are popular for swimming, canoeing, picnicking, fishing, and strolling. But people mainly come here to experience first hand some of what Thoreau wrote about when he spent two years here. Near the park entrance stands a furnished, full-size replica of his tiny cabin, along with a statue of Thoreau and interpretive displays. A cairn marks the site where his cabin stood, accessible by a half-mile trail from the parking area.

The drive rambles south to Wayland, then heads west on US 20—in colonial times the Boston Post Road. A bit more than 5 miles ahead is the turnoff for the ❺ **Wayside Inn** *(Wayside Inn Rd. 978-443-1776. Reservations recommended for lodging and meals).* Inside the big, gambrel-roofed building you'll find a warren of cozy, low-ceilinged rooms, many with fireplaces, and ten upstairs guest chambers. A tavern as early as 1706, the inn became famous—and received its name—when Henry Wadsworth Longfellow wrote *Tales of a Wayside Inn,* a sort of Yankee *Canterbury Tales,* after visiting in 1863. Henry Ford restored the inn in the 1920s and built on the grounds a working gristmill and the nonsectarian Mary-Martha Chapel.

Backtracking on US 20 to South Sudbury, the route then heads north through Stow to Bolton. This portion of the drive takes in attractive country towns and rolling countryside laced with apple orchards.

At Bolton, drive north on Harvard and Bolton Roads to ❻ **Harvard,** where the **Fruitlands Museums** *(102 Prospect Hill Rd. 978-456-3924. Mid-May–mid-Oct. Tues.-Sun.; adm. fee)* recall the story of the utopian experiment undertaken here by A. Bronson Alcott and his followers in 1843-44. They planned to live communally and self-sufficiently, but experience showed them to be better talkers than farmers; they abandoned Fruitlands after seven months. The Fruitlands farmhouse is now a museum of the transcendentalist movement. On the 200-acre grounds are museums of Shaker life, American Indian arts and crafts, and 19th-century American portraits and landscape paintings.

From Harvard, follow Littleton Road to Littleton. Stretch your legs at the **Oak Hill–Tophet Chasm Conservation Land** *(King and Oak Hill Roads off Mass. 110. 978-486-9537).* One trail leads to a swamp within the cliff-enclosed

Beat Generation

Jean-Louis Kerouac became famous for writing about a life lived far from the old textile city of Lowell, Massachusetts, where he was born and raised. But along with Jack Kerouac's beatnik works there stands a solid canon of his books set in Lowell—*The Town and the City, Doctor Sax, Visions of Gerard,* and *Maggie Cassidy.* Many of Kerouac's old homes and haunts still look much the same as when he lived here as a boy in the 1920s and '30s (the houses are private), and his grave is in **Edson Cemetery,** off Gorham Street, 2 miles south of downtown. Ask for a walking tour brochure at the **Lowell National Historical Park Visitor Center** *(978-970-5000).*

chasm, and another climbs up to Summit Rock for views all the way to Boston.

East on Mass. 110 sprawls ❼ **Lowell**★ *(Greater Merrimack Valley Convention & Visitors Bureau 978-459-6150 or 800-443-3332)*, where an expansive downtown district of canals and one-time textile mills has been set aside as **Lowell National Historical Park**★★ *(Visitor Center, 246 Market St. 978-970-5000)*. A film and exhibits at the Visitor Center tell the story of Lowell's planned development as an industrial city in the early 19th century, based on the waterpower of the Merrimack River and its century of prowess as a textile capital. From the center, venture either alone or with a guided tour (in summer, aboard restored trolleys and canal barges) to other park sites. The **Working People Exhibit** *(40 French St. 978-970-5000. Call for schedule)* describes the hard lives of Lowell's immigrant mill workers and Yankee farm girls turned factory hands. A whole floor of working early 20th-century power looms at the **Boott Cotton Mills Museum** *(Foot of John St. 978-970-5000. Adm. fee)* make a racket—and a stream of cotton cloth sold as dish towels in the gift shop. The mill's exhibit on capital, labor, and the organization of Lowell's industries is extremely informative.

91

Looms in Boott Cotton Mills Museum, Lowell

Around the corner on Bridge Street is one of the finest memorials to any writer anywhere. Made of stark steel monoliths, the **Kerouac Commemorative** *(Eastern Canal Park)* bears passages from the works of Lowell native Jack Kerouac (see sidebar p. 90).

Follow Mass. 110 east along the Merrimack River to ❽ **Lawrence** *(Chamber of Commerce 978-686-0900)*, another former textile city. The **Lawrence Heritage State Park** *(Visitor Center, Canal St. at Jackson. 978-794-1655)* offers an excellent perspective on the city's industrial experience, particularly with regard to the 1912 Bread and Roses strike, which galvanized the American labor movement. Its appellation came from a poem by James Oppenheim describing the 25,000 textile workers as striking for basic necessities (bread) plus a little extra (roses). A film fleshes out the history, while vivid interpretive exhibits include a full-size replica of a tenement kitchen.

North Shore ★

75 miles ● 2 days ● Spring through late autumn

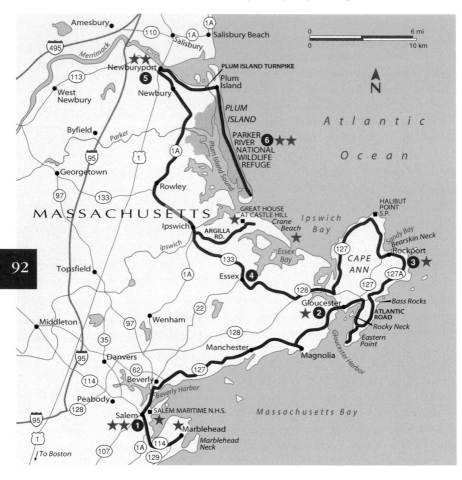

On the map, the drive from Boston to the New Hampshire border looks like a quick hour's run. But east of that highway lies nearly four centuries of history, ranging from some of New England's earliest settlements to the Salem witch trials to the establishment of a Yankee trading empire in the days after the Revolution. There are colonial farmhouses here, along with the castles of Gilded Age magnificoes. Yet for all this human history, the North Shore's beaches and seascapes are among the finest on the East Coast.

The drive begins in Salem, a city associated with one of the darkest episodes and one of the proudest epochs of our history, then continues north along the Boston

Brahmins' 19th-century Gold Coast to the old seafaring city of Gloucester. Rounding Cape Ann, the route skirts the salt marshes of Essex and Ipswich to end at Newburyport, a restored federal-era jewel at the mouth of the Merrimack River.

Settled by Puritan emigrants in 1626 and the capital of the Massachusetts Bay Colony until 1630, ❶ **Salem**★★ *(Chamber of Commerce 508-744-0004)* contains several surviving examples of 17th-century architecture. Perhaps the most famous of these structures is the dark and brooding **House of the Seven Gables**★ *(54 Turner St. 978-744-0991. Adm. fee)*, built in 1668 and immortalized by Salem native Nathaniel Hawthorne. The kitchen re-creates the atmosphere of the house's first period; other rooms appear as they did in Hawthorne's time. Kids love the concealed stairway, possibly used as part of the underground railroad before 1865. Also on the grounds to be explored are Hawthorne's 1804 birthplace (built in 1750) and two additional 17th-century houses.

On the nearby waterfront, the once busy wharves and buildings of the Port of Salem have been preserved as the **Salem Maritime National Historic Site**★ *(174 Derby St. 978-740-1660)*. It commemorates the period, roughly 1783 to 1812, when Salem's merchant princes so successfully plied the China trade that some of their Asian counterparts believed Salem to be a wealthy nation all its own. Begin your tour with the orientation film and exhibits at the **Central Wharf Orientation Center.** Between 1846 and 1849, Hawthorne worked as a port surveyor at the 1819 **Custom House.** And one of America's first millionaires lived at the grand 1762 **Elias Hasket Derby House.**

Hawkes House and Derby House at the Salem Maritime National Historic Site

93

Salem's golden age is also the focus of the **Peabody Essex Museum**★★ *(East India Sq. 978-745-9500. Adm. fee)*, where fine exhibits include marine art and figureheads. Other collections of artifacts span the colonial, federal, and Victorian periods. Included in the admission price are guided tours of four splendid houses dating from the 16th to early 19th centuries, several designed and ornamented by the brilliant federal-era architect Samuel McIntire.

Lined with opulent mansions, many more than 150 years old, **Chestnut Street** has been called the most beautiful street in America. The eclectic collections at the **Stephen Phillips Memorial Trust House** *(34 Chestnut St. 978-744-0440. Late May–mid-Oct. Mon.-Sat.; adm. fee)* include early 19th-century porcelain, horse-drawn carriages, and oriental rugs.

For many visitors, Salem is synonymous with the infamous witch trials of 1692, even though the witch hysteria and persecutions actually began in the nearby town of Danvers, then a part of Salem. Sensational in its sound-and-light effects but quite accurate and sensitive in its overall presentation, the **Salem Witch Museum**★ *(Washington Sq. 978-744-1692. Adm. fee)* tells the sad tale that ended with the deaths of a score of innocent men and women. Judge Jonathan Corwin lived and held preliminary hearings at the 1642 **Witch House** *(310 1/2 Essex St. 978-744-0180. Mid-March–early Dec.; adm. fee)*. With its steep roof, overhanging second story, and diamond-paned windows, the house is notable more as an architectural survivor than for its witch trial associations.

Jutting into the Atlantic 4 miles southeast of town is **Marblehead**★ *(Chamber of Commerce 781-631-2868)*. Here resides one of America's most celebrated icons, one so deeply etched into our national consciousness that it's almost surprising to see it exists on canvas. Painted by Archibald M. Willard in 1876, the "Spirit of '76"—the famed portrait of three bloodied but unbowed Revolutionary War stalwarts—hangs in the Selectmen's Meeting Room of **Abbot Hall** *(Washington St. 781-631-0000. June-Oct.; donations)*. Nearby, the Marblehead Arts Association exhibits local works at the Georgian **King Hooper Mansion** *(8 Hooper St. 781-631-2608. Adm. fee)*. The Georgian **Jeremiah Lee Mansion** *(161 Washington St. 781-631-1069. Adm. fee)* houses the town historical society's collections of

Hanging figures at the Witch Dungeon Museum, Salem

pre- and post-Revolutionary War period furnishings.

The drive backtracks through Salem to Mass. 127, where it veers toward Cape Ann. In this skein of quiet towns, Boston Brahmins—the aristocratic heirs of the merchant princes—built their summer homes. Just off Mass. 127 in **Magnolia,** the early 20th-century inventor John Hays Hammond created **Hammond Castle** ★ *(80 Hesperus Ave. 978-283-7673. Call for schedule; adm. fee)* to showcase his medieval collections and classical antiquities. An amalgam of parts from real European castles, the great stone structure also features an enormous pipe organ and fine sea views.

Fisherman's monument in Gloucester

Follow Mass. 127 into ❷ **Gloucester** ★ *(Chamber of Commerce 978-283-0455),* a harbor town whose fortunes have ridden with its fishing fleet for the past three and a half centuries. On Western Avenue, the **Gloucester Fisherman** peers forever out to sea, his bronze hands clutching a bronze wheel. A dedication remembers "they that go down to the sea in ships, 1623-1923." Indeed, over the years 10,000 Gloucestermen have never come back.

The story of Gloucester's rich seafaring tradition is told at the **Cape Ann Historical Museum** *(27 Pleasant St. 978-283-0455. Tues.-Sat. Closed Feb.; adm. fee).* The modern museum also features Revere silver, Chinese porcelain, and an entire gallery of works by the mid-1800s luminist Fitz Hugh Lane.

Leaving downtown Gloucester, branch off Mass. 127A to explore the winding streets of **Rocky Neck,** a waterfront warren thick with artists' studios and galleries. Then head out to **Eastern Point,** where collector and interior designer Henry Davis Sleeper spent the early years of this century building **Beauport** ★ ★ *(75 Eastern Point Blvd. 978-283-0800. Mid-May–mid-Sept. Mon.-Fri., daily mid-Sept.–mid-Oct. Call for tour schedules. Adm. fee),* a turreted, shingled monument to his own eclectic tastes. The rambling, 40-room indulgence (27 rooms are on the tour) is the ultimate pack rat house, a succession of *objet*-rich chambers that chronicle the changes in American taste from early colonial through China trade grandeur and beyond. Having finished a tour, no one unfamiliar with the house could possibly retrace his steps.

Take Atlantic Road along the ocean, past rugged Bass Rocks and several sandy swimming beaches, to rejoin

North Shore

Great Ipswich Fright

They called it the Great Ipswich Fright. It happened on April 20, 1775, when, in the excitement after Lexington and Concord, a rumor spread that British troops had landed on the North Shore. As word went around that they were approaching Ipswich, fear spread up the coast with near impossible speed. The terror raced north through Rowley, past Newbury, into Amesbury and Salisbury, and across the New Hampshire border. Entire settlements were emptied of their inhabitants, who fled with such commotion their northern neighbors thought they were the advancing enemy.

Like a flood tide, the terror receded by the following day. No one had sacked Ipswich; no red-coated pursuers were racing north toward the Merrimack. Essex County's yeomen and their families drifted back to their homes and farms, wiser in the ways of what a later age would call mass psychology.

Mass. 127A and head into ❸ **Rockport**★ *(Chamber of Commerce 978-546-6575)*. The compact cluster of shops and galleries around Rockport Harbor culminates in **Bearskin Neck,** a narrow spit of land busy with artisans and seafood shops. **Motif #1,** a red fisherman's shack standing out over the water, is a subject so beloved by artists that it was entirely rebuilt following the Great Blizzard of 1978. Next, follow Mass. 127 around Cape Ann's northern tip to **Halibut Point State Park** *(Gott Ave. 978-546-2997)*. Here, the open Atlantic crashes against the granite headlands that gave Rockport its name.

Loop back toward Gloucester along Cape Ann's northern coast, then take Mass. 128 and Mass. 133 west to ❹ **Essex.** Small but disproportionately endowed with antique shops and seafood restaurants, Essex huddles at the edge of a vast network of salt marshes and tidal creeks; the town boasts no fewer than 57 clam flats. Along with shellfishing, the traditional town business was shipbuilding. Between 1668 and 1949, 3,000 to 4,000 schooners slid down the ways at Essex shipyards. Dioramas, hands-on exhibits, and films at the **Essex Shipbuilding Museum** *(28 and 66 Main St. 978-768-7541. Mid-May–mid-Oct. Thurs.-Mon.; adm. fee)* help laymen sort out the bewildering variety of sailing vessels. Kids can try their hand at caulking, boring, and fastening planking to frames with the wooden dowels called treenails (pronounced TRUN-nels).

Mass. 133 joins Mass. 1A just south of **Ipswich** *(Chamber of Commerce 978-356-3231)*, a town that gave its name to clams and its exurbanite character to the stories of former resident John Updike. Turn right on Argilla Road to reach the grandest of all the North Shore's summer houses, the **Great House at Castle Hill**★ *(978-356-4351. May–Oct. Wed.-Thurs. p.m.; adm. fee)*. Once belonging to Chicago plumbing fixture magnate Richard Crane, the 59-room mansion is a Jacobean-style English country house with a decidedly New England view: A half-mile allée directs the eye to the ocean and New Hampshire and Maine's faraway Isles of Shoals. Barrier dunes hide the great swath of sand and sea of adjoining **Crane Beach**★ *(Parking fee)* from the rest of the world, making it ideal for swimming and sunbathing.

In Ipswich center, two fine houses represent two distinct eras. The **Whipple House** *(1 Village Green. 978-356-2811. May–mid-Oct. Wed.-Sun.; adm. fee)* evolved between 1655 and 1700; its massive welcoming hearths, steep sheltering gables, and fortresslike windows typify this early period of colonial architecture, as does the collection of local furnishings within. Across the street, the 1795 federal **Heard House** *(54 S. Main St. 978-356-2641. May–mid-Oct. Wed.-Sun.; adm. fee)* is altogether different in spirit. Its styling bespeaks the confidence and prosperity of the China trade years; exquisite Oriental furnishings and art-works form the bulk of its collections.

The China trade and, later, the clipper ships drove the economy of ❺ **Newburyport**★★ *(Chamber of Commerce 978-462-6680),* located 12 miles north at the mouth of the Merri-mack River. At the 1834 **Custom House Maritime Museum** *(25 Water St. 978-462-8681. April-Dec.; adm. fee),* ship models, marine documents, and stern portraits of sea captains recall the little city's golden age. One room celebrates Newburyport author John P. Marquand. From here stroll to Market Square and **State Street,** whose tidy brick commercial buildings were all built after an 1811 fire and restored in 1970. The show-place of Newburyport's mercantile upper crust, **High Street**★

is a virtual gallery of impeccably restored federal-period houses, rivaled only by Salem and Portsmouth, New Hampshire. One is the impressive **Cushing House Museum** *(98 High St. 978-462-2681. May-Oct. Tues.-Sat.; adm. fee),* whose sumptuous interior offers a perfect picture of patrician domestic life in the days when Yankee traders owned the seas.

Motif #1 in Rockport

Before heading back toward the Boston area via US 1 (or I-95), take the Plum Island Turnpike southeast to the ❻ **Parker River National Wildlife Refuge**★★ *(978-465-5753. Entrance fee).* Over 4,500 acres of salt marshes, scrub forest, barrier dunes, and unspoiled beach along the southern two-thirds of Plum Island comprise the federally protected property. Birding opportunities here are among the East Coast's finest, with chances to spot more than 300 species of birds, including loons, egrets, and kestrels.

South Shore ★

100 miles ● 3 days ● Spring through fall ● Many attractions close in winter.

This seaside drive winds down the Bay State's quiet, largely residential coastline that stretches along Massachusetts and Cape Cod Bays. It begins with a glimpse into the domestic lives of one of America's most distinguished families, passes through a string of trim colonial towns, and pauses at the place where New England settlement began. It ends at two old coastal cities with a rich seafaring tradition.

Beginning just south of Boston in Quincy, the drive rambles south on Mass. 3A, the main highway of colonial times but now a side road largely superceded by the Mass. 3 expressway farther inland. At Plymouth the route cuts inland to rejoin the coast at Wareham, on the other side of Cape Cod's narrow shoulder, then wanders west to the waterfronts of New Bedford and Fall River.

❶ **Quincy** *(Chamber of Commerce 617-479-1111)* came by its nickname City of Presidents early on. The town is the ancestral home of the Adams family, which produced the second and sixth chief executives of the United States. The **Adams National Historic Site** ★★ *(Visitor Center, 1250 Hancock St. 617-770-1175. Mid-April–mid-Nov.; adm. fee for guided house tours)* recounts the family's story. Shuttle buses leave from the downtown Visitor Center for tours of three Adams-related sites: the **John Adams Birthplace**, a 1681 frame structure that was the seat of a 180-acre farm when John Adams was born here in 1735; the **John Quincy Adams Birthplace,** next door, where John Adams's son was born in 1767 and where the elder Adams drafted the

Massachusetts constitution in 1779; and the **Old House,** the home purchased by John Adams in 1787, which remained in the family until 1927. Largest and most completely furnished of the three dwellings, the Old House showcases portraits and possessions of four generations of Adamses, including diplomat Charles Francis Adams and historians Henry and Brooks Adams. Also on the beautifully landscaped grounds, the 1872 **Stone Library** houses the 14,000-volume collection amassed by John Quincy Adams.

99

Old House and gardens at the Adams National Historic Site, Quincy

In downtown Quincy, **Hancock Cemetery** *(Hancock St.),* dating from about 1640, contains the graves of Adamses going back as far as Henry Adams, who emigrated from England about 1636. The two Presidents were originally interred here, but now rest across the street in the crypt of the Greek Revival **United First Parish Church** *(1306 Hancock St. 617-773-0062. Tours mid-April–mid-Nov.; adm. fee).* Pick up a cemetery map at the church.

The drive moves southeast from Quincy on Mass. 3A to **Weymouth,** where the **Abigail Adams Birthplace** *(North and Norton Sts. 781-335-1067. July–Labor Day Tues.-Sun. p.m. and by appt.; adm. fee)* recounts the remarkable life of the wife and trusted adviser of John Adams. The daughter of Rev. William Smith and his wife, Elizabeth, Abigail was born in 1744 in the small parsonage, which dates from 1685. Period furnishings show how the gambrel-roofed house might have looked in her childhood.

A few miles east rests the old colonial town of **Hingham,** settled in 1635. Among the town's many early American houses and public buildings is the 1681 **Old Ship Church** *(90 Main St. 781-749-1679. Sun. service 10:30 a.m. or visit by appt.),* believed to be the nation's oldest house of worship in continuous use. Probably named for the shiplike construction of its roof frame, the church—now Universalist—is unusual for its square shape; inside, diamond-paned windows cast filtered light on stark exposed beams and old-fashioned box pews. Behind the

First Parish Meeting House, dating from 1747, Cohasset

church, the old burial ground has several Lincoln graves; Samuel Lincoln, an early ancestor of Abraham Lincoln, worshiped at the Old Ship Church.

In colonial days, travelers could obtain a hot meal and a pint of ale a short distance away at the circa 1680 **Old Ordinary** *(21 Lincoln St. 781-749-0013. Mid-June–Labor Day Tues.-Sat.; adm. fee)*. Its 14 rooms now house the Hingham Historical Society's fine collections of period furniture and glass.

Bear left off of Mass. 3A onto Summer Street and take a left on Martin Lane for the 251-acre **World's End Reservation** *(Trustees of Reservations 781-821-2977. Adm. fee)*, located on a grassy, hilly peninsula that juts into Hingham Bay. The views of Boston and its water approaches are spectacular, and 4 miles of pathways make for fine, leisurely strolling.

Just ahead, Nantasket Avenue winds along Hingham Bay to the town of **Hull** *(Chamber of Commerce 781-925-9980)*, which occupies its own elbowed peninsula protecting Hingham Bay from Massachusetts Bay. Hull's Nantasket Beach was once the site of Paragon Park, a popular amusement center. The last remaining ride, the 1928 **Carousel Under the Clock** *(205 Nantasket Ave. 781-925-0472. Daily in summer; weekends only spring and fall; adm. fee)* flaunts gaily painted horses and a Wurlitzer organ.

Near the tip of the peninsula, photographs and old-time equipment at the **Hull Lifesaving Museum** *(1117 Nantasket Ave. 781-925-LIFE. July-Aug. Wed.-Sun., June and Sept. weekends only; adm. fee)* recall the days when brave men rowed stout surfboats to offshore shipwrecks. Housed in an old lifesaving station, the museum has one room set up as the living and dining quarters for rescuers of a century ago. Just uphill from the museum lies **Fort Revere Park** *(Telegraph Hill. 781-925-1778. Adm. fee)*, where a water tower that once served a coastal defense site commands views of Boston and the sea. A small museum tells about local fortifications dating from Revolutionary War times.

Leaving Hull, turn left on Jerusalem Road, which winds along the open Atlantic and offers breathtaking views of the solitary Minots Ledge Light. Soon you'll enter **Cohasset,** whose maritime heritage dates back to 1614, when John Smith landed here during an exploration voyage. An 18th-century ship chandlery houses the **Cohasset Historical Society Maritime Museum** *(4 Elm St. 617-383-6930. June-Sept. Tues.-Sun.; adm. fee),* full of harpoons, mackerel jigs, ship's bells, scrimshaw, and lots more relating to the days when Cohasset was a bustling fishing town. Next door, the society's 1810 **Captain John Wilson House** is furnished in period style.

In ❷ **Scituate,** the next town along Mass. 3A, First Parish Road passes the unusual **Lawson Tower** *(June-Sept. second Sundays; adm. fee).* A turn-of-the-century millionaire neighbor, who thought the original 153-foot water tower ugly, had it refurbished to resemble a shingled medieval German watch tower. Along with the view, the tower offers music from a ten-bell chime, played occasionally. Nearby, photographs, books, and period furniture at the **Cudworth House** *(617-545-1083. First Parish Road. Mid-June–mid-Sept. Wed.-Sat. or by appt.; adm. fee)* detail the lives of early town settlers. The 1797 saltbox farmhouse boasts a cattle pound where neighbors could come claim their stray cattle, a restored barn filled with handmade tools and carriages, and a 250-year-old loom (on which weaving demonstrations are given periodically).

Farther south, **Marshfield** *(Chamber of Commerce 617-834-8911)* is home to the 1699 **Winslow House** *(Webster and Careswell Sts. 617-837-5753. Mid-June–mid-Oct. Wed.-Sun.; adm. fee),* a rambling structure that's actually a series of connected 17th- and 19th-century buildings. Three centuries of furnishings reflect the same long period in the lives of its locally prominent owners. On the grounds stands the small building that Daniel Webster used as a law office. Webster lived in Marshfield for the last 20 years before his death in 1852. Some of the great stateman's letters and papers on nature and farming, as well as other possessions, are on display. Webster is buried a few miles away in bucolic **Winslow Cemetery** *(Winslow Cemetery Rd.).*

Fruit of the Pilgrims

Monument above Plymouth Rock, Plymouth

A few miles south the route arrives at the serene seaside town of **Duxbury** *(Greater Plymouth Area Chamber of Commerce 508-830-1620)*. About 1627, John Alden, Myles Standish, and other Pilgrims seeking grazing lands for their cattle arrived here, on land once occupied by Indians. John and Priscilla Alden—celebrated in Longfellow's poem "The Courtship of Myles Standish"—resided in the foursquare, center-chimney 1653 **Alden House** *(105 Alden St. 781-934-9092. Late June–Labor Day Tues.-Sun., weekends only mid-May–late June and Labor Day–mid-Oct.; adm. fee)*. Both Aldens, along with Myles Standish and other first settlers, lie in the **Old Burying Ground** *(Chestnut St.)*. A statue of Captain Standish stands atop the 116-foot granite **Standish Monument** *(Standish Park. Mem. Day–Labor Day weekends)*, where a climb up the interior staircase is rewarded by vistas reaching from Boston's skyline to the tip of Cape Cod.

Duxbury's prosperous federal period is recalled in the 1808 yellow-shingled **King Caesar House** *(120 King Caesar Rd. 781-934-6106. Mid-June–Labor Day Wed.-Sun., Fri.-Sat. rest of year; adm. fee)*, built by local shipbuilder and merchant prince Ezra Weston, Jr. French wallpapers, elegant furnishings, and graceful corner chimneys reflect the magnificent style of living that went with his nickname, King Caesar.

On the way into Plymouth, you may wish to stop at the **Cranberry World Visitor's Center** *(225 Water St. 508-747-2350. May-Nov.)* to learn all about *Vaccinium macrocarpon*, one of only three native American fruits. The lowlands around Plymouth are prime cranberry country, and this exhibit, sponsored by Ocean Spray Cranberries Inc., covers planting, harvesting, and recipes.

The premier South Shore destination, ❸ **Plymouth** ★ *(Chamber of Commerce 508-830-1620)* is America's hometown. Right in the heart of the city sits **Plymouth Rock** *(Water St.)*, traditionally recognized as the landing place of the *Mayflower* Pilgrims in 1620. Above the tide-washed rock, with a walkway for viewing, stands a neoclassical canopy designed by McKim, Mead & White. Just a short walk away, the ***Mayflower II*** ★ *(Water St. 508-746-1622. April-Nov.; adm. fee also covers admission to Plimoth Plantation)*

Lepidopterist's Delight

Located inland just south of Plymouth, **Myles Standish State Forest** *(Camping information 508-866-2950)* sprawls across hundreds of acres of pine barrens that form a habitat for many species of unusual moths. Lepidopterists come here at night in hopes of catching *Catocala herodias gerhardi, Harrisimemna trisignata, Zale horrida,* or other prizes. If you see someone smearing a sweet-smelling concoction on a tree around twilight, don't be puzzled: it's moth bait.

is permanently moored. Launched in England in 1956, this full-size reproduction of the *Mayflower* sailed to Plymouth the following year. Complete with 17th-century accents, the sailors and passengers on board are dressed in Pilgrim garb and represent historical persons from the 1620 voyage. The result is the closest thing we have to a live, first-person narrative of the passage.

Pilgrim furniture, weapons, and armor at the **Pilgrim Hall Museum**★ *(75 Court St. 508-746-1620. Closed Jan.; adm. fee)* comprise the country's largest collection of Pilgrim-era artifacts. Here you'll also find Bibles belonging to John Alden and William Bradford, as well as articles believed to have been carried on the *Mayflower*.

Three appropriately furnished Plymouth houses provide a glimpse into the austere lifestyle of early settlers. The son of an original Pilgrim lived in the circa 1667 **Howland House** *(33 Sandwich St. 508-746-9590. Mem. Day–Columbus Day; adm. fee).* The pre-1640 **Richard Sparrow House** *(42 Summer St. 508-747-1240. Thurs.-Tues.; adm. fee)* is the oldest existing wooden frame house in Plymouth. And the 1677 **Harlow Old Fort House and Heritage Craft Center** *(119 Sandwich St. 508-746-0012. July-Aug. Tues.-Sat.; June Thurs.-Sat.; Sept.–mid-Oct. Fri.-Sat.; adm. fee)* may have been built from the timbers of the original Pilgrim fort. Pilgrim-era furnishings and artifacts offer insight into the Pilgrims' lives. Spinners, weavers, and candlemakers in period dress demonstrate early crafts.

Set on a seaside hilltop just south of modern Plymouth, **Plimoth Plantation**★★ *(Plimoth Plantation Hwy. 508-746-1622. April-Nov.; adm. fee)* replicates the Pilgrims' first primitive settlement in the year 1627. Behind a timbered palisade, 20 or so tiny, weathered houses cluster around a wooden blockhouse. Flowers and herbs sprout in small garden plots, pigs roam nearby pens, and cornstalks grow in cultivated fields. Costumed villagers go about their daily business, but will stop to talk about their pioneer lives (and feign no knowledge of anything later than 1627).

103

Mayflower II in Plymouth

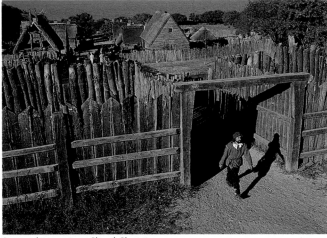

Costumed interpreter at Plimoth Plantation

Wampanoag Indians helped the Pilgrims survive the early settlement years by teaching them to live off the land. At the plantation's **Hobbamock's Homesite,** a typical single-family Wampanoag Indian dwelling made of bark and reeds, guides plant and cook and depict the crafts of dugout canoe-making, basketry, weaving, and other traditional Native American activities.

Leaving Plymouth, the drive continues south on US 44, Mass. 58, and Mass. 28 to ❹ **Wareham,** a small town on Buzzards Bay. The **Fearing Tavern Museum** *(Elm St. at Mass. 28. 508-295-6839. July-Aug. Thurs.-Sun. and by appt.; adm. fee)* harks back to the days when the village tavern was a post office, town hall, courtroom, stagecoach stop, and watering hole.

Follow US 6 south and west along Buzzards Bay to **New Bedford** ★ *(Historic District Visitor Center, Williams St. 508-991-6200 or 800-508-5353),* the mainland headquarters of America's 19th-century whaling industry. Today, the town claims New England's largest fishing fleet. To stroll along the historic waterfront—still a workaday neighborhood for New Bedford's nearly 2,000 commercial fishermen—pick up a walking tour brochure at the **Waterfront Visitor Center** *(Old Pier 3. 508-979-1745).* Among the many 19th-century houses and commercial buildings that line the narrow streets stands the 1834 granite **Custom House,** still in use. When it's in port, be sure to visit the schooner *Ernestina* *(State Pier. 508-992-4900),* built in 1894.

In the nearby historic Johnny Cake Hill neighborhood, the principal attraction is the **New Bedford Whaling Museum** ★ ★ *(18 Johnny Cake Hill. 508-997-0046).* The museum's exhaustive collections include harpoons, an actual whaleboat, whale oil lamps and candles, a complete humpback whale skeleton, whalebone carvings, scrimshaw, and a model of the 1826 whaling ship *Lagoda,* said to be the world's largest model of such a ship. A fascinating 1922 documentary whaling film is shown regularly.

Across the street stands the **Seamen's Bethel** (*15 Johnny Cake Hill. 508-992-3295. If locked, ring bell at Mariner's Home next door*), the whalers' chapel that Herman Melville made famous in *Moby Dick*. Poignant memorials to lost seamen line the chapel's walls.

In another part of town, the **Rotch-Jones-Duff House** (*396 County St. 508-997-1401. Tues.-Sun.; adm. fee*) depicts a different aspect of the whaling era. This Greek Revival mansion belonged to a succession of merchant princes, and its furnishings and gardens reveal just how lucrative whaling was for those who owned the ships and reaped the rewards.

The drive ends farther west in the old mill city of

5 Fall River (*Chamber of Commerce 508-676-8226*). Massive granite cotton mills that stand in and around the city center serve as stark monuments to the town's once vibrant and now defunct cotton industry that in 1911 produced 3 miles of cloth per minute. More modern history can be

found at Battleship Cove, where four historic ships and a submarine are docked. The centerpiece is the **U.S.S. *Massachusetts*** ★ (*508-678-1100. Adm. fee*), the 46,000-ton World War II battleship that served as one of two flagships for Operation Torch, the 1942 invasion of North Africa. Visitors can spend hours on several decks of the vast ship, climbing into antiaircraft gun turrets, marveling at the silent strength of the 16-inch guns, and touring the bridge, engine room, and magazines.

Navy ships at Battleship Cove, Fall River

Also moored here and open to visitors are the destroyer ***Joseph P. Kennedy, Jr.,*** the submarine ***Lionfish,*** and the only two PT boats displayed anywhere.

The nearby **Marine Museum at Fall River** (*70 Water St. 508-674-3533. Adm. fee*) recalls maritime experiences of a different sort. Exhibits depict the 90-year era of travel between New York and Fall River on the elegant steamers of the Fall River Line and tell the ever fascinating story of the R.M.S. *Titanic*. Memorabilia from the *Titanic* includes a deck chair, Mrs. J. J. Astor's life jacket, and the 28-foot model used in a 1953 movie based on the disaster.

Cape Cod ★★

**160 miles ● 3 to 4 days (not counting the islands)
● Spring through fall; weather fine in winter but
most attractions closed ● Traffic can be heavy in
summer, especially on weekends.**

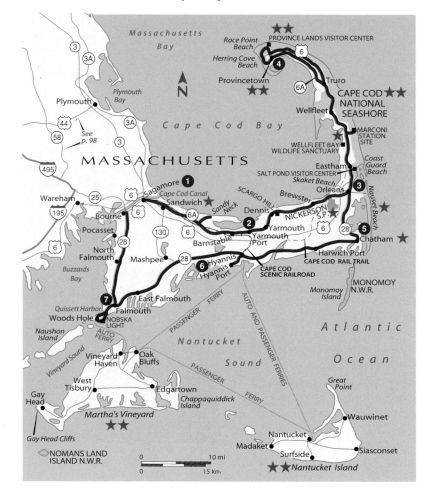

There are capes all along the New England coast, but when anyone talks of "the Cape," the meaning is immediately clear. This drive takes in virtually all of Cape Cod, from the quiet villages along the bay side to the beautifully desolate dunelands of the outer Cape's national seashore, from lively Provincetown to the busy resorts that face Nantucket Sound.

The drive begins at the Cape Cod Canal and follows Mass. 6A along the contour of Cape Cod Bay to the armlike Cape's "elbow," beyond which the narrow lower Cape (actually farther north than the landward upper Cape) braces against the North Atlantic. Stopping along the ocean side and at Provincetown, the route turns south back to Orleans, then meanders out to Chatham before following southerly Mass. 28 to Hyannis and Falmouth. Ferry connections at Hyannis or Woods Hole offer the option of a side trip to the islands of Nantucket and Martha's Vineyard.

After crossing the Sagamore Bridge, the first town you reach is ❶ **Sagamore.** The **Pairpoint Crystal Company** *(Mass. 6A. 508-888-2344. Workshop closed weekends)* carries on the local tradition of hand-blowing lead crystal into functional and decorative items. Visitors can watch artisans blow, shape, and finish glassware.

Farther east lies the oldest town on the Cape, **Sandwich**★ *(Chamber of Commerce 508-759-6000).* Settled by Puritans in 1637, the town flourished in the 19th century as a glassmaking center. The many kinds of decorative and table glass—clear and colored, blown and pressed, cut and engraved—made Sandwich famous. The **Sandwich Glass Museum** *(129 Main St. 508-888-0251. Daily April-Oct., Wed.-Sun. rest of year; adm. fee)* preserves much of the best work from all different eras. Reproductions are available in the gift shop.

A short distance away, across Sandwich's tree-shaded village center, stands

Glassware at the Sandwich Glass Museum

the beautifully proportioned **Hoxie House** *(18 Water St. 508-888-1173. Mid-June–Sept.; adm. fee).* The structure dates from about 1675, and may very well be the Cape's oldest saltbox house. Also dating from the 17th century, the adjacent water-powered **Dexter Grist Mill** *(Main and Water Sts. Contact Chamber of Commerce 508-759-3122. Mid-June–mid-Sept.; adm. fee)* still turns out delicious stone-ground cornmeal, which can be purchased on site.

On nearby Shawme Pond, the **Thornton W. Burgess Museum** *(4 Water St. 508-888-6870. Daily April-Dec., Jan.-March Tues.-Sat.; donations)* honors the Sandwich native who wrote "Peter Cottontail" and other classic animal stories for

Former U.S. Coast Guard Station, Eastham

children. The author's colonial-era house contains early editions, original Harrison Cady illustrations, correspondence, nature exhibits, and a gift shop filled with Burgess books.

Set on the manicured grounds of a former estate just outside town, the **Heritage Plantation of Sandwich** ★ (*Grove and Pine Sts. 508-888-1222. Mid-May–late Oct.; adm. fee*) showcases all kinds of Americana in a complex of reconstructed historic buildings. Among the many exhibits, you'll find a working 1912 carousel, Currier & Ives lithographs, military firearms, and one of the nation's finest collections of classic automobiles. A look at Gary Cooper's 1930 Duesenberg alone is worth the price of admission (and a good deal more).

The drive wends about 5 miles farther east to Sandy Neck Road. Turn left here for **Sandy Neck** (*508-362-8306. Parking fee in summer*), a splendid barrier beach of low, rolling dunes and gentle waters. A 6.2-mile trail meanders through gorgeous isolation to Sandy Neck Light.

Just ahead on Mass. 6A is **Barnstable,** settled in 1639. For years, the settlement thrived on fish caught in the Great Banks. In the 19th century, hundreds of sea captains lived in town; many of their houses still stand. For a glimpse into the town's past, stop by the **Donald G. Trayser Memorial Museum** (*Mass. 6A. 508-362-2092. June–mid-Oct. Tues.-Sun.; adm. fee*), Barnstable's unofficial attic.

Mass. 6A leads next to the part of Yarmouth called ❷ **Yarmouth Port** (*Chamber of Commerce 508-778-1008*). Long-time resident Mary Thacher bequeathed her collection of 17th-, 18th-, and 19th-century furniture, along with the 1780 **Winslow Crocker House** (*Mass. 6A. 508-362-4385. June–mid-Oct. Tues., Thurs., Sat.-Sun.; adm. fee*), to the Society for the Preservation of New England Antiquities. Nearby, the Oriental treasures carried home by its sea captain owner fill the 1840 **Captain Bangs Hallet House** (*11 Strawberry Ln. 508-*

362-3021. July-Aug. Thurs. and Sun.; June, Sept., and Oct. Sun. only; adm. fee), a side-entrance Greek Revival dwelling.

Locals gather for breakfast and lunch at the postage stamp-size **Hallet's Store** *(Mass. 6A. 508-362-3662),* complete with a marble counter, old-fashioned soda fountain, and tiers of wooden shelves. If it's sunbathing you want, head to **Gray's Beach** *(End of Centre St. 508-775-7910),* reached via a quarter-mile boardwalk across a salt marsh and tidal inlet.

Follow Mass. 6A seven miles east to **Dennis.** A hard right on Scargo Hill Road leads to one of Cape Cod's highest points, a 160-foot bump on the landscape called **Scargo Hill.** Then climb the stone tower's 38 steps for an all-encompassing view of the Cape's thrusting arm and the sea on either side.

Though **Brewster** *(Chamber of Commerce 508-255-7045),* some 4 miles ahead, has no harbor, many 19th-century sea captains made their homes here. Some of their grand old houses still edge the leafy streets off Mass. 6A. The **Cape Cod Museum of Natural History** *(Mass. 6A. 508-896-3867. Adm. fee)* serves up the Cape that is often forgotten beneath its vacation veneer. Sea urchins, diamondback terrapins, and many other local creatures reside in marine and freshwater viewing tanks. Outside, nature trails reveal a variety of Cape ecosystems.

A mile down the road, some of the fire-fighting equipment displayed at the indoor-outdoor **New England Fire and History Museum** *(Mass. 6A. 508-896-5711. Late May–mid-Oct.; adm. fee)* dates from colonial days.

Cape Cod's most expansive inland preserve, Brewster's **Nickerson State Park★** *(Mass. 6A. 508-896-3491. Camping fee),* to the east of town, encompasses nearly 2,000 acres of gently rolling pine forest dotted with freshwater ponds. Here you can camp, hike, swim, fish for trout, and bike ride; a park trail connects with the 25-mile **Cape Cod Rail Trail,** a paved-over railbed. Bikes may be rented nearby.

Mass. 6A meets US 6 near ❸ **Orleans** *(Chamber of Commerce 508-240-2484),* supposedly named after the Duke of Orleans,

109

Cape Cod clambake

Nauset Beach, Orleans

who visited here after the French Revolution. Some of the Cape's best beaches edge the town's bay and ocean shores. On the calm bay side, **Skaket Beach** *(West Rd. to Skaket Beach Rd. Fee for town sticker)* has a gentle drop-off and hundreds of yards of exposed sandbar at low tide. On the ocean side at **Nauset Beach**★ *(Main St. to Beach Road. Fee for town sticker)*, the bracing Atlantic waters create a rougher surf, and the surf casting is excellent when the stripers and bluefish are running.

The drive now enters scrubby pitch pine and oak forest, leading to a lonely, sandy world of beaches, sea cliffs, and dunes cloaked in bayberry and heath. A good portion of this beautiful place has been preserved as the 43,557-acre **Cape Cod National Seashore**★★. At the **Salt Pond Visitor Center** *(508-255-3421. Daily March-Dec., Jan.-Feb. weekends only)* near Eastham, park roads wander to two fine beaches. The Nauset Marsh Trail leads through oak and pine to a salt marsh.

Farther along, trails and boardwalks lace nearly 1,000 acres of pine woods, marshes, and tidal creeks at the Massachusetts Audubon Society's **Wellfleet Bay Wildlife Sanctuary**★ *(508-349-2615. Visitor Center closed Mon. in winter; adm. fee)*. Whimbrels and Yellowlegs are two of the more than 200 species of birds that have been spotted here. Nature center exhibits include tanks of native fish and reptiles.

Just ahead, an outdoor exhibit at the **Marconi Station Site** *(Off US 6)* commemorates the cliff-top spot where radio pioneer Guglielmo Marconi transmitted the first message across the Atlantic in 1903. A Marconi station operated here until 1917; among the signals picked up were distress calls from the R.M.S. *Titanic* in 1912.

At the quiet residential town of **Truro,** bear left onto Mass. 6A, the scenic bay-side approach to the popular summer resort town of **❹ Provincetown★★** *(Chamber of Commerce 508-487-3424).* A picturesque jumble of narrow streets, this old colonial seaport possesses elements of a Portuguese fishing village. The Pilgrims landed here in 1620, before settling on their final destination of Plymouth. The stop is commemorated by the **Pilgrim Monument & Provincetown Museum★** *(High Pole Hill Rd. 508-487-1310. Daily April-Nov. Call for winter schedule; adm. fee),* a 252-foot Italian Renaissance granite tower erected in 1910. The spectacular 360-degree view at the top shows off the Cape's variegated landscape and the sea beyond. Ship models, whaling equipment, and other maritime artifacts fill the museum near the monument's base.

Local history remains the focus at the **Provincetown Heritage Museum** *(356 Commercial St. 508-487-7098. Mid-June–mid-Oct.; adm. fee),* which peels back the town's many historical and cultural layers; there's even a half-scale model of a Grand Banks fishing schooner.

Perhaps the most dramatically beautiful portion of the national seashore can be found at the nearby **Province Lands.** Stop by the **Province Lands Visitor Center★★** *(Race Point Rd. 508-487-1256. Closed in winter)* for information. A short climb to the observation deck provides majestic views of dune, village, and sea. For an up-close, beach-plum-and-bayberry-level look, hiking trails meander through the dunes. Or rent a bike in Provincetown and ride through the dunes and scrub forests on a 5-mile bike trail loop. Province Lands also has two fine white-sand beaches: **Herring Cove** and **Race Point.** At Race Point Beach, the **Old Harbor Life Saving Museum** *(Race Point Rd. 508-487-1256. July-Aug., call for hours in spring and fall; adm. fee)* tells about the heroics of the old U.S Lifesaving Service at one of its most challenging outposts.

Leaving Provincetown, the drive follows US 6 to Orleans. From the traffic rotary here, follow Mass. 6A and Mass. 28 north (though the road actually goes south) to **❺ Chatham★** *(Chamber of Commerce 508-240-2484 or 800-715-5567),* at the Cape's outer elbow. Smaller and more sedate than Provincetown, Chatham nevertheless offers plenty of shop and gallery browsing, as well as splendid sea views from the overlook at **Chatham Light** *(End of Main St.).* Tucked among the 18th- and 19th-century houses of its

Native cranberries

Nantucket Island ★★

Nantucket *(Chamber of Commerce 508-228-1700)* lies 30 miles out at sea, where the stark fact of the North Atlantic is always close at hand. Inland Nantucket is mostly beautiful moorland, though no place is really "inland" on this small island, a ragged, beach-fringed arc roughly 14 by 3.5 miles. The only real town is Nantucket, which has been painstakingly preserved to reflect its stature as the world whaling capital in the early 1800s. Visit the **Whaling Museum** for a thorough perspective on the world of Ahab and Ishmael; the **Hawden House** to see how the money from whale oil and spermaceti was spent; and the **Old South Church,** a federal-era masterpiece with a trompe l'oeil interior. The **Oldest House** (1686) has an almost medieval countenance, and the **Maria Mitchell Science Center** honors a pioneer American astronomer born on the island in 1818. See ferry information p. 113.

111

leafy residential neighborhood is pleasant **Chase Park**
(Cross St.). Here you'll find a 1797 **gristmill** and the historical society's **Old Atwood House Museum** *(347 Stage Harbor Rd. 508-945-3642. Mid-June–Sept. Tues.-Fri.; adm. fee)*.
Victorian furniture, Sandwich glass, and seafarer tools fill
the 1752 gambrel-roofed house. But the museum's greatest treasure is in a separate gallery out back—a series of
murals by artist Alice Stallknecht Wight depicting the
Chatham people she knew in the early to mid-1900s: at
their daily occupations, at a town supper, and listening to
the preaching of Christ, dressed like one of them.

Leaving Chatham, amble westward alongside Nantucket Sound. In the 1960s the seaside quarter of

Gay Head Cliffs on Martha's Vineyard

Hyannis Port, in the village of ❻ **Hyannis,** became one
of the world's most famous addresses. The era is recalled
at the **John F. Kennedy Hyannis Museum** *(397 Main St.
508-790-3077. Daily in summer, Wed.-Sat. in winter; adm. fee)*,
not a museum really but an extensive gallery of large-
format photographs that capture the 35th President's lifelong romance with the Cape. Kennedy is also remembered at the **John F. Kennedy Memorial** *(Ocean St.)*, a
harbor-side fountain and reflecting pool.

Hyannis is the point of departure for the **Cape Cod**

Scenic Railroad *(252 Main St. 508-771-3788. June-Oct. Tues.-Sun. Reserve for dinner trains. Fare)*, which runs scenic excursions and dinner trains to Sandwich and Sagamore.

Ferries for **Martha's Vineyard**★★ and **Nantucket Island**★★ (see sidebars p. 111 and this page) depart regularly from Hyannis. Hy-Line boats *(Ocean St. Dock. 508-778-2600. May–Oct.; fare)* ferry passengers and bike riders to both islands. And the Steamship Authority *(South Street Dock. 508-477-8600. Mid-March–Oct. Car reservations necessary. Fare)* takes passengers and cars to Nantucket only.

The drive proceeds farther west to ❼ **Falmouth,** the Cape's southwesternmost point. Settled by Congregationalists in the early 1660s, the town became a whaling and shipbuilding center in the 19th century. Clustered around the classic village green are the 1796 **First Congregational Church,** with its graceful steeple and Paul Revere bell, and two historic house museums belonging to the **Falmouth Historical Society** *(55-65 Palmer Ave. 508-548-4857. Mid-June–mid-Sept. Mon.-Fri.; adm. fee).* Furnishings, toys, and medical equipment at the 1790 **Julia Wood House** reflect the changing tastes of the four different families who lived here over nearly 150 years. Among the various collections at the adjacent **Conant House Museum** are mementos of Katherine Lee Bates, the Falmouth native who wrote "America the Beautiful."

From Falmouth green, take Woods Hole Road south onto a narrow spur of land to Oyster Pond Road and turn left. At Beach Road turn right and follow the shoreline to Nobska Point and the 1828 **Nobska Light,** whose penetrating beam can be seen 17 miles out at sea. Just ahead, when you come to Woods Hole Road again, turn left. Nearby is the famous **Woods Hole Oceanographic Institution** *(15 School St. 508-289-2252. Daily Mem. Day–Labor Day; Tues.-Sun. May, Sept., and Oct.; Fri.-Sun. April, Nov., and Dec.; adm. fee),* founded in 1930. Its Exhibit Center showcases the various activities and discoveries of its scientists.

Go north on Quisset Road to the town of **Woods Hole.** Here, the Steamship Authority *(508-477-8600. Car reservations necessary; fare)* offers year-round ferry service to both Martha's Vineyard and Nantucket.

As you return north to Falmouth and to the mainland beyond, pause for a moment at tranquil **Quissett Harbor,** a haven for pleasure boats.

Martha's Vineyard★★

Martha's Vineyard *(Chamber of Commerce 508-693-0085)* has acquired a considerable reputation as a celebrity resort in recent years, but at heart it still seems like a bit of New England countryside surrounded by saltwater—especially if you visit in spring or fall. There are several towns. In yachty **Edgartown,** with its handsome federal and Greek Revival houses, visit the **Dukes County Historical Society Museum** for a look at the Vineyard's past, and the 1672 **Vincent House,** oldest on the island. Bustling Vineyard Haven offers the **Seaman's Bethel;** built over 100 years ago, it houses maritime exhibits. **Oak Bluffs'** trademark is the **Camp Meeting Grounds,** a toylike cluster of colorful Victorian gingerbread cottages built by Methodist camp meeting participants. Don't miss America's oldest working carousel, the Flying Horses. Besides its many beaches, the Vineyard's most striking natural attraction is **Gay Head Cliffs,** where sunset turns clay and sand into a mineral rainbow as the surf crashes below. See ferry information on this page.

113

Providence and the Coast ★

**150 miles ● 2 to 3 days ● Spring through fall
● Avoid Providence at rush hour.**

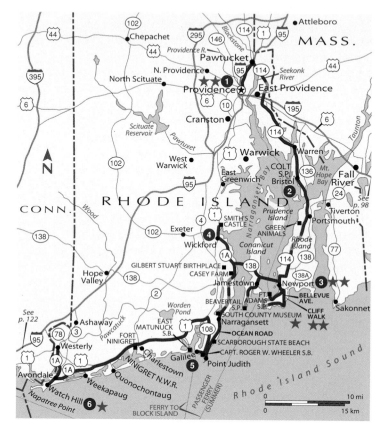

Rhode Island may be America's smallest state, but it possesses one of the country's most convoluted coastlines. Divided into eastern and western portions by the jagged thrust of island-strewn Narragansett Bay, Little Rhody is a place where the chowdermaker never has far to go for clams.

This drive begins in the state capital and chief city, Providence, then trails along the bay's east shore and onto its biggest island, Rhode Island itself. Leaving the posh resort of Newport, the route hopscotches onto quieter Conanicut Island, then follows Block Island Sound by way of fishing ports and white-sand beaches to the Victorian summer outpost of Watch Hill.

Back in 1636, after squabbling with Puritans over religious freedom and being exiled from Massachusetts, Roger

Williams settled ❶ **Providence**★★ *(Convention and Visitors Bureau 401-274-1636)* on the Providence River. In a 4.5-acre park near the original site of his plantation, the **Roger Williams National Memorial** *(282 N. Main St. 401-521-7266)* features a comprehensive orientation center with exhibits on the freedom of belief. Within easy walking distance are the sites that dot **College Hill,** a combination university, art school, and residential neighborhood. Lovely Georgian and federal mansions line Benefit Street, including the 1810 **Sullivan-Dorr House** *(Private)* at number 109. An astonishingly broad collection at the nearby **Rhode Island School of Design Museum of Art**★ *(224 Benefit St. 401-454-6501. July–Labor Day Wed.-Sat.; Tues., Wed., Fri., and Sat. rest of year; adm. fee)* ranges from Egyptian antiquities to American period rooms to French Impressionists. Edgar Allen Poe once browsed the stacks at the **Providence Athenaeum** *(251 Benefit St. 401-421-6970. Mon.-Fri., call about Sat.-Sun. hours),* an 1836 members' association library. Farther up the hill is the campus of **Brown University** and its **John Hay Library** *(20 Prospect St. 401-863-2146. Mon.-Fri.),* whose upper-floor gallery displays a wonderful collection of toy soldiers in uniforms from all eras. Several blocks off campus, the 1786 **John Brown House**★★ *(52 Power St. 401-331-8575. Tues.-Sun., closed Jan.-Feb.; adm. fee)* belonged to the wealthiest of the 18th-century Brown brothers, whose family named the university.

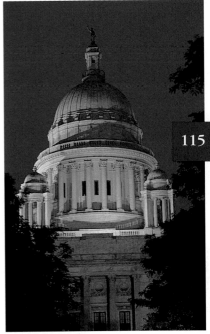

State Capitol, Providence

Downtown, on the west side of the Providence River, stands the **Arcade** *(Between Westminster and Weybosset Sts.).* There's nothing unusual about most bi-level indoor shopping malls, but this one was created by Greek Revival architects in 1828 and remains in use! Farther west rises the **Federal Hill** neighborhood, probably the most intensely Italian quarter in New England next to Boston's North End. Bring an appetite for pasta and Chianti; the restaurants here aren't nouvelle Italian.

Watching over all is the **Rhode Island State Capitol** *(82 Smith St. 401-277-2357. Mon.-Fri.; call for guided tour schedule).* Architects McKim, Mead & White completed the

Bobbins in a store window,
Slater Mill Historic Site, Pawtucket

building in 1904, after nine years of construction, and topped it with the world's fourth largest self-supported dome. The ornate Gilded Age interior displays an interesting combination of state mementos, including the 1663 Royal Charter from King Charles II.

The American industrial revolution was born just up the river in **Pawtucket.** At the **Slater Mill Historic Site**★ *(167 Roosevelt Ave. 401-725-8638. June-Oct. Tues.-Sun.; March-May and Nov.-Dec. weekends only; adm. fee),* antique textile machinery clatters away on the very spot where, in 1793, Englishman Samuel Slater introduced the first successful water-powered cotton spinning factory to the United States. A 16,000-pound waterwheel still operates at the nearby Wilkinson Mill, where Slater's machinery was built.

Head south on R.I. 114 along the eastern shore of Narragansett Bay to ❷ **Bristol** *(Chamber of Commerce 401-245-0750),* where the **Herreshoff Marine Museum** *(1 Burnside St. 401-253-5000. May-Oct.; adm. fee)* recalls a proud nautical tradition. For more than 80 years Herreshoff was one of the world's premier yacht builders;

Slater Mill Historic Site, Pawtucket

eight of its yachts defended the America's Cup title between 1893 and 1934. Forty boats are on display.

A short drive less than a mile south leads to the **Blithewold Mansion and Gardens**★ *(House open April-Oct. Tues.-Sun.; adm. fee).* Built in 1907 by a Pennsylvania coal baron who took a liking to Bristol when he came to buy a Herreshoff yacht, the 45-room seaside mansion sits amid 33 exquisitely landscaped acres. Try and visit when they are in bloom.

R.I. 114 leads onto the island called Rhode and into the town of **Portsmouth.** Here, on the grounds of another handsome old estate, you'll find the elaborate topiary garden known as **Green Animals** (*380 Cory's Ln. 401-847-1000. May-Oct.; adm. fee*). Wander among whimsical pruned living creations, including such shrubby beasts as a teddy bear, giraffe, elephant, and camel, as well as geometrical figures and ornamental designs dating from about 1880.

R.I. 114 continues to the tip of the island and the storied little city of ❸ **Newport**★★ (*Newport County Convention and Visitors Bureau 401-849-8098 or 800-326-6030*), which has led varied and brilliant lives as a prosperous colonial seaport, Gilded Age showplace, and yachting capital.

Clustered around Newport Harbor, colonial Newport lives on in a number of 17th- and 18th-century structures. Newport's oldest house, the circa 1675 **Wanton-Lyman-Hazard House** (*17 Broadway. 401-846-3622. Call for hours; adm. fee*), belonged to an outspoken Loyalist who was hanged in effigy for enforcing the Stamp Act. A graceful steeple rises above nearby **Trinity Church** (*Queen Anne Sq. 401-846-0660. Daily June-Oct.; May, June, Sept., and Oct. Sun.-Fri.; Nov.-April Sun. only*), dating from 1726. Be sure to look inside at the Christopher Wren-inspired interior. Prime examples of Newport-made furniture fill the 1748 **Hunter House**★ (*54 Washington St. 401-847-1000. Daily in summer, April and Oct. Sat.-Sun.; adm. fee*), a Georgian upper middle-class house. And the Georgian **Touro Synagogue** (*85 Touro St. 401-847-4794. Mem. Day–mid-Oct. Sun.-Fri.; Sun. only rest of year; year-round by appt.*), built in 1763, is North America's oldest synagogue. George Washington proclaimed America's commitment to religious freedom here about 1790.

The **Old Stone Mill** (*Touro Park*) claims title as downtown Newport's strangest edifice. Although historians generally think the 24-foot stone tower dates back no earlier than colonial times, its peculiar design and the absence of a construction record have contributed to the popular belief that Vikings erected it a thousand years ago.

Newport's gaudiest and most legendary epoch is represented by the fabulous string of summer "cottages" on and around Bellevue Avenue. The **Preservation Society of Newport County**★★ (*424 Bellevue Ave. 401-847-1000. Call for individual house schedules. Varying admission fees apply to different combination house tours, including Hunter*

Johnnycakes

One of Rhode Island's more famous culinary contributions is the johnnycake, made from locally grown, stone-ground white cornmeal. In colonial times these little corn flapjacks—called "journey" cakes—were handy portable nourishment. A common recipe calls for a cup of white cornmeal, a teaspoon each of salt and sugar, a cup of boiling water, and a half cup of milk. Mix the dry ingredients together and gradually stir in the boiling water. Thin with the milk until the mixture resembles a thick pancake batter, then cook on a greased griddle over moderate heat, turning once until brown on both sides. Johnnycakes are best served hot, split, and buttered—and you don't have to be going on a journey to eat them!

117

House and Green Animals in Portsmouth) maintains the finest of these palatial summer residences. Largest and perhaps most extravagant is Cornelius Vanderbilt II's **The Breakers** *(Ochre Point Ave.)*, built in 1895. Its design by Richard Morris Hunt reflects the style of Italian Renaissance palaces. Cornelius's brother, William, also employed Hunt to build his 1892 indulgence, an extravaganza of marble aptly named **Marble House** *(Bellevue Ave.)*.

At the turn of the century, Pennsylvania coal baron Edward J. Berwind modeled **The Elms** *(Bellevue Ave.)* after an 18th-century Parisian château. William S. Wetmore's **Château-sur-mer** *(Bellevue Ave.)*, built in 1852 and enlarged 20 years later, masses around a 45-foot-high great hall. Two other magnificent houses maintained by the preservation society include 1839 **Kingscote** *(Bellevue Ave.)*, a fine example of Richard Upjohn's Carpenter Gothic style, and 1902 **Rosecliff** *(Bellevue Ave.)*, designed by Stanford White to resemble the Grand Trianon at Versailles.

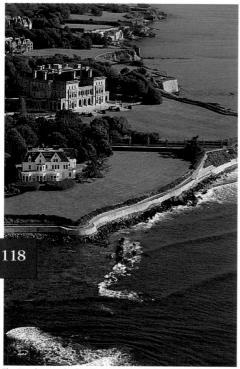

The Breakers and other "cottages" on Ochre Point, Newport

For fine exterior views of these elite retreats and the ocean, follow the 3.5-mile seaside **Cliff Walk★★,** which extends from Easton's Beach to Bailey's Beach. You can get a good look at the mansions from just past the end of Narragansett Avenue.

An estate with more recent associations of wealth and privilege is **Hammersmith Farm** *(Ocean Dr. 401-846-0420. April–mid-Oct.; adm. fee)*, a rambling bay-side mansion set in grounds landscaped by Frederick Law Olmsted. Site of Jacqueline Bouvier's wedding to John F. Kennedy in 1953, it later served as a summer White House.

The remains of an 19th-century fort built to defend Newport Harbor stand at nearby **Fort Adams State Park** *(Harrison Ave. 401-847-2400. Adm. fee Mem. Day–Labor Day)*. Visitors can tour its powder magazines and tunnels. Also at the park, the in-water boat collection and America's Cup gallery at the **Museum of Yachting** *(Ocean Dr. 401-847-1018. Daily mid-May–mid-Oct.; adm. fee)* tell about

Newport's glory
days of yacht racing.
During the summer
you can cruise over
to Block Island
(Ferry 401-783-4613.
See page 121 for infor-
mation on the island)
on a no-vehicle pas-
senger ferry that
departs from
the park.

Newport sailing regatta

The **International Tennis Hall of Fame and Museum**
(Newport Casino, 194 Bellevue Ave. 401-846-4567. Adm. fee)
chronicles the history of another sport with strong Newport ties. From 1881 to 1914, the National Lawn Tennis
Championships took place on grass courts at this site.

The drive continues west on R.I. 138 to Conanicut
Island and **Jamestown,** a quiet, almost semirural community that seems a world away from Newport. Overlooking
the bay, 280-acre **Watson Farm** *(455 North Rd. 401-423-
0005. June–mid-Oct. Tues., Thurs., and Sun.; adm. fee)* has
been a working farm for two centuries. Today visitors can
observe traditional crop raising and animal husbandry
techniques. Just down the road, the weathered, gray-
shingle **Jamestown Windmill** *(N. Main St. 401-423-3650.
Mid-June–mid-Sept. weekends; adm. fee),* built in 1787 to grind
cornmeal, is still cranked up on special occasions. At the
island's windblown southern tip, **Beavertail State Park** *(S.
Main St. 401-353-8822)* offers isolation, splendid views, and
the **Beavertail Lighthouse Museum** *(401-423-3650. Mid-
June–Aug. Wed.-Sun.; adm. fee),* which tells you about the
lonely business of lighthouse keeping.

Follow R.I. 138 across the Jamestown Bridge to the
mainland, where R.I. 1A leads north to ❹ **Wickford,** a
tidy village of shop-lined streets. Just north of town on
Wickford Cove stands **Smith's Castle** *(US 1. 401-294-3521.
June-Aug. Thurs.-Mon., May and Sept. Fri.-Sun., and by appt.;
adm. fee).* Built in 1678, the venerable structure was the
headquarters of a 27-square-mile plantation during the
early 1700s. Inside, its old beams and wide-planked floors
provide the perfect setting for rare period furnishings.

Return south through Wickford on R.I. 1A and follow
signs for the **Gilbert Stuart Birthplace** *(815 Gilbert Stuart*

Rd., Saunderstown. 401-294-3001. Apr.-Nov. Thurs.-Mon.; adm. fee). The artist was born here in 1755, four years after the dwelling was built. Set beside a lovely little millpond, the home is decorated with period furniture and tools. Stuart's father built the nearby snuff mill, where a 2,000-pound water-wheel runs the mill and acts like a mortar and pestle to grind the tobacco. A short distance south is the circa 1750 **Casey Farm** *(R.I. 1A. 401-295-1030. June–mid-Oct. Tues., Thurs., and Sat.; adm. fee for house),* a colonial farmstead still surrounded by pastures and vegetable fields. The house holds exhibits as well as 18th-century furnishings. You can buy organic produce and herbs in season.

Downtown Wickford

Follow R.I. 1A to just before the Narragansett Pier, where the **South County Museum**★ *(R.I. 1A. 401-783-5400. May-Oct. Wed.-Sun.; adm. fee)* interprets Rhode Island rural life from 1800 through the 1930s. Some 10,000 artifacts furnish such authentic settings as a general store, carpentry shop, and country kitchen. Across the road stands the entrance to **Narragansett Town Beach** *(401-789-1044. Summer; parking fee),* a fine stretch of sand on Rhode Island Sound. Continue into **Narragansett** and bear left beneath the arch that connects two massive stone towers—all that remains of a McKim, Mead & White-designed casino that burned down in 1900. The left-hand tower houses a Visitor Center *(401-783-7121).*

Once past the towers, stay on Ocean Road to reach **Scarborough State Beach** *(401-789-8031. Summer; parking fee),* one in a string of superbly maintained white-sand beaches. A few miles beyond lies **Point Judith** *(Chamber of Commerce 401-783-7121),* with its working lighthouse and U.S. Coast Guard station. From here you'll have to turn around and head back north on R.I. 108, passing the entrance to **Captain Roger B. Wheeler State Beach** *(401-789-3563. Summer; parking fee),* which faces Block Island Sound's open waters.

Farther north, another turnoff leads to ❺ **Galilee,** where wharves—for commercial fishing boats, lobster boats, fishing party boats, and pleasure craft—seem to outnumber dry-land structures. Several spots invite you to enjoy a seafood dinner while watching the harbor activity.

Among the vessels that dock at Galilee, the **Block Island ferry** *(Interstate Navigation Co. 401-783-4613. Schedules vary with season. Car reservations necessary; fare)* takes just over an hour to reach one of New England's most isolated and timeless destinations. Located 12 miles out at sea, 11-square-mile **Block Island**★★ *(Block Island Chamber of Commerce 401-466-2982 or 800-383-2474)* offers windswept moors, woodlands and wildflowers, long stretches of unspoiled beach, quiet country lanes for bicycling, ponds visited by a stunning variety of birds, and a harbor village with Victorian hotels.

Continuing on from Galilee, take R.I. 108 north to US 1, which veers south past the turnoffs for several fine beaches, including Jerusalem's **East Matunuck State Beach** *(Snug Harbor turnoff to the end of Succotash Beach Rd. 401-789-8585. Summer; parking fee)*. At **Charlestown** *(Chamber of Commerce 401-364-3878)*, scant stone foundation ruins of the 17th-century Dutch **Fort Ninigret** *(US 1)* overlook a tranquil cove. Ahead, on the south side of US 1, the 404-acre **Ninigret National Wildlife Refuge** *(401-364-9124)* includes salt marsh and barrier beach environments. You can see a variety of waterfowl and, during the fall migration season, you may even spot a bald eagle.

Several miles farther, bear left on R.I. 1A to reach Rhode Island's westernmost and southernmost point, ❻ **Watch Hill**★ *(Chamber of Commerce 401-596-7761 or 800-732-7636)*. Enormous turn-of-the-century, shingled summer houses look down over Watch Hill's harbor and waterfront main street, lined with shops and seafood restaurants. At the far end stands one of seacoast Rhode Island's most endearing icons, the **Flying Horse Carousel** *(Bay St. 401-596-7761 or 800-732-7636. Mid-June–Labor Day; adm. fee)*. Near the carousel you can enter Watch Hill's town beach and hike 1.5 miles to sandy **Napatree Point,** a narrow spit of barrier beach preserved as a conservation area. For effortless sea viewing, your best bet is the grand colonnaded veranda at the **Ocean House** *(2 Bluff Ave. 401-348-8161. Late June–Labor Day)*, a wooden ark of a hotel built in 1868 that is a classic of its genre.

Return to US 1 and the town of Westerly via R.I. 1A, which is designated "1A South" on road signs, even though you'll be driving due north.

70 miles ● 2 to 3 days ● Spring through fall ● Accommodations in New Haven are difficult to obtain at beginning and end of Yale school year. ● In peak summer season, try to visit Mystic on weekdays.

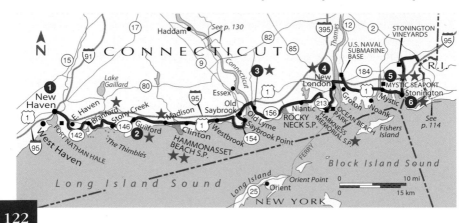

Escaping the gravitational pull of New York City, this passage up the Connecticut coast along the strip of water known as Long Island Sound takes in a string of old Yankee towns still devoted to their maritime heritage. Some simply carry on much as they have for the past couple of hundred years, while others are using cutting-edge technology to shape the future of marine exploration and industry.

Beginning in New Haven, the drive rambles almost due east on secondary roads south of I-95 to Stonington, one of New England's loveliest coastal villages. Along the way, it visits the historic towns of Branford, Old Lyme, and New London, as well as Mystic Seaport. All the while keep an eye to the east, where the imperturbable waters of the sound form the backdrop to this drive.

The Puritans who founded ❶ **New Haven** *(Greater New Haven Convention and Visitors Bureau 203-777-8550 or 800-332-7829)* in 1638 constructed their settlement on a grid pattern of nine equal squares including a central common. Today's New Haven, a busy center of education and industry, sprawls far beyond its original boundaries, but **New Haven Green**★ remains intact.

An important commercial port in the early 19th century, New Haven is now best known as the home of **Yale University**★★ *(203-432-2300. Free guided tours leave from Yale Visitor Information Center, 149 Elm St. Mon.-Fri. at 10:30 a.m. and 2 p.m., and Sat.-Sun. at 1:30 p.m.)*, founded in 1701.

Yale University, New Haven

As a student, Nathan Hale roomed in the school's oldest original building, the Georgian **Connecticut Hall,** built in 1752; a statue in front of the building honors the Revolutionary War martyr. Be sure to visit the **Beinecke Rare Book and Manuscript Library** *(121 Wall St. 203-432-2977. Closed Sun. year-round and Sat. in Aug.),* whose extensive collection includes a Gutenberg Bible and a folio of original Audubon prints. Note the building's 250 translucent marble panels that protect the books from direct sunlight and ultraviolet rays. Then walk over to the **Peabody Museum of Natural History** *(170 Whitney Ave. 203-432-5050. Adm. fee)* and examine its superb collections, including exhibits on extinct species of North American flora and fauna, the history and culture of ancient Egypt and Mexico, and dinosaur fossils.

For spectacular views of New Haven Harbor, visit two adjacent reconstructed forts: the Revolutionary War **Black Rock Fort** and the Civil War **Fort Nathan Hale** *(Woodward Ave. 203-946-8790. Mem. Day–Labor Day).*

Leaving town, head east to **East Haven,** where you can hop a 3-mile vintage trolley ride at the **Shore Line Trolley Museum** *(17 River St. 203-467-6927. Daily Mem. Day–Labor Day; weekends in May, Sept., and Oct., Sun. only in April; adm. fee).* Among the nearly 100 cars stands No. 500, a parlor car with hand-carved and inlaid oak woodwork, as well as an 1895 electric car said to have inspired the comic strip "Toonerville Folks," carried in major newspapers between 1915 and 1955.

In **Branford**★ *(Chamber of Commerce 203-488-5500),* 18th- and 19th-century buildings cluster around the magnificent town green. Nearby stands **Harrison House**★ *(124 S. Main St. 203-488-4828. June-Sept. Thurs.-Sun. p.m.),* a restored 1724 classic saltbox filled with period furnishings.

Windsurfer off Lighthouse Point near New Haven

Farther east, watch for the turnoff to the picture-perfect harbor village of **Stony Creek** and **The Thimbles,** a group of some 350 islands. Just 23 are inhabited, and a few appear only large enough to support their one or two houses. Legend says that Captain Kidd buried his pirate booty on one of the outcrops. **Summer sight-seeing tours**★ leave from the Stony Creek dock. Try Sea Mist Thimble Island Cruise *(203-488-8905)*, Volsunga Thimble Island Cruise *(203-488-9978)*, or Connecticut Sea Ventures *(203-397-3921)*.

Following the shoreline northeast, Conn. 146 leads to ❷ **Guilford**★, one of New England's prettiest towns—with one of the prettiest greens. Tree-lined streets are graced by a trove of beautifully kept houses (most privately owned) dating from the early colonial period through the 19th century. Pick up a walking tour brochure at the Visitor Center *(32 Church St.)*, and wander down to New England's oldest stone house, built by the town's founder in 1639 and now the **Henry Whitfield State Museum**★ *(248 Old Whitfield St. 203-453-2457. Wed.-Sun.; adm. fee)*. Many changes have been made over the years, but a carefully executed 1930s restoration gives visitors a sense of how Connecticut's earliest English settlers lived. Indeed, many of the 17th- and 18th-century antiques inside once belonged to Guilford's first families. The garden is being replanted with an assortment of 17th-century vegetables, flowers, and medicinal herbs.

Henry Whitfield State Museum, Guilford

Two colonial saltboxes are also open to the public. The circa 1660 **Hyland House** *(84 Boston St. 203-453-9477. June–Labor Day Tues.-Sun., Labor Day–Columbus Day weekends only; adm. fee)* has unusual interior woodwork and three walk-in fireplaces outfitted for 17th-century cooking. Inside the circa 1774 **Thomas Griswold House** *(171 Boston St. 203-453-3176. Mid-June–Labor Day Tues.-Sun., Labor Day–Oct. weekends only; adm. fee)* you'll find a local history museum, and outside you'll see a blacksmith shop and colonial garden.

Before continuing east on US 1, take a short detour west to **Bishop's Orchards** *(203-453-2338; "Pick Your Own" info 203-453-6424)*, where there's always something to pick, from strawberries in June to Christmas trees in December.

About 6 miles east of Guilford lies the lovely colonial town of **Madison**★ *(Chamber of Commerce 203-245-7394)*.

In addition to the magnificent town green, be sure to visit the 1785 **Allis-Bushnell House Museum** ★ *(853 Boston Post Rd. 203-245-4567. Mem. Day–Sept. Wed., Fri., and Sat. p.m.).* Once owned by Cornelius Bushnell, who financed the building of the iron-clad *Monitor* during the Civil War, the museum presents period furnishings, costumes, glassware, and a telegram sent by President Lincoln requesting nine more vessels just like the *Monitor.*

Just east of town stretches **Hammonasset Beach State Park** ★★ *(203-245-2785. Adm. fee in season),* the largest state shoreline park, complete with a fabulous 2-mile-long beach, nature center, concession stand, and bathhouses. The best ocean views are from **Meigs Point.**

In **Clinton,** the circa 1790 **Stanton House** ★ *(63 E. Main St. 203-669-2132. June-Sept. Tues.-Sun. p.m.; donations)* remained in the Stanton family until 1916. It's filled with their furnishings and possessions, including a superb collection of antique American and Staffordshire dinnerware. The attached general store looks just as it did when Adam Stanton—and later his son—ran it from 1804 to 1864.

A repository of war memorabilia and military vehicles, books, music, and videos, the **Military Historians Headquarters-Museum** *(N. Main St. 860-399-9460. Tues.-Fri. or by appt.)* in **Westbrook** also holds the largest collection of American military uniforms in the country. The fourth weekend in August the town hosts the annual **Westbrook Muster** *(860-399-6436),* with performances by 45 to 50 fife and drum corps.

Along the way to **Saybrook Point** and the mouth of the Connecticut River, Great Hammond Road and Conn. 154 loop past pristine wetlands, quaint summer cottages, and beautiful views of Long Island Sound. At waterside, plaques on display in the nearly 18-acre **Fort Saybrook Monument Park** *(Saybrook Point. 203-395-3152)* tell the story of Saybrook Colony, one of the state's oldest settlements, as well as one of New England's earliest military fortifications. A boardwalk overlooking the salt marsh offers fine vistas for bird-watching.

Fishermen at Meigs Point, Hammonasset Beach State Park

Popular with summer vacationers, **Old Saybrook** *(Chamber of Commerce 203-388-3266)* is the state's second oldest officially chartered town. Yale College convened here until 1716. The Georgian circa 1767 **General William Hart House** *(350 Main St. 203-388-2622. Mid-June–mid-Sept. Sat.-Sun. p.m.)* has interesting transfer-print tiles, elegant paneling, and a superb herb garden.

I-95 leads across the Connecticut River toward the quiet, tree-shaded streets of ❸ **Old Lyme**★. Samuel Belcher designed the town's beautiful **First Congregational Church of Old Lyme** *(2 Ferry Road),* built in 1816-17, as well as the 1817 Florence Griswold House. Now the **Florence Griswold Museum**★ *(96 Lyme St. 860-434-5542. June-Nov. Tues.-Sun. and Dec.-May Wed.-Sun.; adm. fee),* the late Georgian mansion is as renowned for its place in American art history as it is for its collection of American paintings. Willard Metcalf and Childe Hassam are two of the many artists who stayed at Miss Florence's boarding-house in the early 1900s, when they came to paint the Connecticut countryside. By the turn of the century, the Griswold home was a vibrant art colony—first serving as the cradle of the American Barbizon movement, then playing a pivotal role in the rise of American impression-

Impressionist paintings at Florence Griswold Museum, Old Lyme

ism. The dining room, its door and wall panels painted by artist-boarders, is spectacular. The restored studio of American impressionist William Chadwick is also here.

In a Victorian mansion across town, artist Elizabeth Tashjian has launched a different kind of movement—to give nuts their proper due. Her **Nut Museum** *(303 Ferry Rd. 860-434-7636. May-Oct. Wed., Sat., and Sun. p.m.; donations plus one nut),* features nut paintings, nut masks, nut sculptures, and other creations.

Next, treat yourself to an elegant meal at the 1756 **Bee and Thistle Inn** *(100 Lyme St. 860-434-1667 or 800-622-4946. Closed Tues.)* or the nearby 1850s Victorian **Old Lyme Inn** *(85 Lyme St. 860-434-2600. Closed first two weeks in Jan.).*

Leaving town, Conn. 156 meanders along the shore-line to **Rocky Neck State Park** *(860-739-5471. Mem. Day–*

Labor Day; adm. fee), where the nearly mile-long crescent beach offers fabulous swimming, fishing, and picnicking.

In **Niantic,** every inch of the **Children's Museum of Southeastern Connecticut** *(409 Main St. 860-691-1255. Closed Mon. during school year; adm. fee)* is packed with fun stuff for kids to touch, play with, and learn about. The museum is small and popular, so be prepared for lots of good-natured noise.

Cross the Niantic River and head south on Conn. 213 to **Harkness Memorial State Park**★ *(275 Great Neck Rd. 860-443-5725. Day-use fee Mem. Day–Labor Day),* overlooking Long Island Sound. The mansion is closed for renovations at least through 1996, but the gardens are fine for strolling, and the beach offers sunbathing and fishing. In July and August, Summer Music Inc. presents concerts on Saturdays and three weekdays (phone park for information).

Farther ahead, our route passes the **Eugene O'Neill Theater Center** *(305 Great Neck Rd. 860-443-5378. Call for summer schedule; adm. fee),* dedicated to the exploration and development of new works in the theater. Every piece is a work in progress, mostly for adult audiences.

Watch for Ocean Avenue, which leads to **Ocean Beach Park** *(860-447-3031 or 800-510-SAND. Mem. Day–Labor Day; adm. fee).* In addition to some of the best ocean swimming in the area, you'll find a freshwater swimming pool, water slides, a great boardwalk, miniature golf, and an arcade.

In 1646 colonial governor John Winthrop, Jr., founded ❹ **New London**★ *(Chamber of Commerce 860-443-8332)* on the Thames River. Owing to its deep natural harbor, the town soon became a major colonial seaport, and from 1794 to 1899, the nation's third largest whaling port. Nobel Prize-winning playwright Eugene O'Neill (1888-1953) spent his first 27 summers at **Monte Cristo Cottage** *(325 Pequot Ave. 860-443-0051. Mem. Day–Labor Day. Call ahead for days and times; adm. fee)* and drew from experiences here in writing *Ah, Wilderness!* and *Long Day's Journey into Night.*

To best see the numerous downtown sites, go by foot; pick up a walking tour brochure at one of the shops. Be sure to stop at the **Hempsted Houses**★ *(Hempstead and Jay Sts. 860-443-7949. Mid-May–mid-Oct. Thurs.-Sun. p.m.; adm. fee),* two structures that provide a fascinating look at early New London life. The 1678 **Joshua Hempsted House,** the town's oldest surviving house and one of New England's oldest frame buildings, was occupied

Lighthouses

The Connecticut coast is dotted with lighthouses, including eight designated as historic. These beacons, built in the 1800s, shine out at Stonington Harbor in Stonington, New Haven Harbor and Southwest Ledge in New Haven, Saybrook Breakwater and Lynde Point in Old Saybrook, New London Harbor and New London Ledge, and Morgan Point in Noank. Southwest Ledge and Morgan Point, along with lighthouses in Greenwich, Norwalk, Fairfield, and Stratford in western Connecticut, are the occasional destinations for boat trips. For tour information and a brochure, contact the Lighthouse Preservation Society (800-727-BEAM).

Sailor statue along State Street, New London

continuously by Hempsteds until 1937. It has been faithfully restored according to descriptions found in Joshua's diary, kept from 1711 to 1758. The adjacent stone **Nathaniel Hempsted House** was built in 1759 by Joshua's grandson. Inside, period antiques and family heirlooms provide a glimpse into that time.

Located within the hillside campus of the U.S. Coast Guard Academy, the **U.S. Coast Guard Museum** *(15 Mohegan Ave. 860-444-8511)* uses a portion of its collection of 6,000 works of art and artifacts to help document the history of the U.S. Coast Guard since its founding in 1790. Outside, the tall-masted training ship *Eagle* can be toured when in port. Call for a schedule of military reviews and concerts.

The collection at the **Lyman Allyn Art Museum**★ *(625 Williams St. 860-443-2545. Tues.-Sun.; adm. fee)* spans 5,000 years and five continents and includes Connecticut impressionist paintings, silver items by New London craftsmen, and tribal arts from Africa.

Cross over the Thames River on I-95 and take the Conn. 12 exit at **Groton** north to the **U.S.S. *Nautilus*** ★ *(U.S. Naval Submarine Base. 860-449-3174 or 800-343-0079. Closed briefly in spring and winter for routine maintenance),* the first nuclear-powered submarine. Built and launched here in 1954, the *Nautilus* shattered every submerged speed and distance record and sailed to the North Pole. The adjacent **Submarine Force Museum** ★, a repository for U.S. Submarine Force records, has exhibits on submarine history, three working periscopes, and an operating control room.

In 1781 British troops under the command of Benedict Arnold defeated a small number of Connecticut militiamen under the command of Col. William Ledyard. When Ledyard surrendered, he and more than 80 of his men were murdered. The massacre is commemorated at the South Groton site, now **Fort Griswold Battlefield State Park** *(Monument St. and Park Ave. 860-455-1729. Monument and museum closed weekdays Labor Day–Columbus Day).*

Aboard **EnviroLab** *(Univ. of Conn. Avery Point Campus. 860-445-9007. Summer only; adm. fee),* visitors use nets and scientific instruments to learn about the marine environment. Reservations are required for the 2.5-hour cruises. EnviroLab also offers trips out to the **New London Ledge Light.**

Continue east on US 1 to **Mystic** *(Shoreline Visitor Information Center 860-536-1641),* a thriving 19th-century seaport and major shipbuilding center before it became Connecticut's second largest tourist destination (after the casinos). The town's—and America's—maritime history is brought to life at ❺ **Mystic Seaport**★★ *(75 Greenmanville Ave. 860-572-5315. Adm. fee)*. Historic ships and exhibit galleries help illustrate the impact of whaling and maritime trade on the nation's economic, social, and cultural life. Several vessels are open for touring, including the *Charles W. Morgan*, America's last surviving wooden whaling ship. Book early in the day to ride one of several boats, including the S.S. *Sabino*, the country's last coal-fired passenger steamer.

Did you know a beluga whale eats about 18,250 pounds of fish a year? Can you identify African blackfooted penguins? These are just a few things to learn at the **Mystic Marinelife Aquarium**★★ *(55 Coogan Blvd. 860-572-5955. Adm. fee)*, an extensive indoor-outdoor complex with sharks, Pacific octopuses, and the nation's only display of Steller sea lions. Beluga whales and Atlantic bottlenose dolphins provide entertainment in the Marine Theater.

129

A few miles away Conn. 1A dips south to ❻ **Stonington**★, an early shipbuilding center whose character is preserved in lovely old houses lining leafy streets. Fishing is still an important industry here and tools of the trade— past and present—are displayed at the **Old Lighthouse Museum** *(7 Water St. 860-535-1440. Daily July-Aug.; Tues.-Sun. May-June and Sept.-Oct.; adm. fee)*, built in 1823 and the first government-operated lighthouse in the state. From North Main Street, take Pequot Trail Road/Taugwonk Road north to **Stonington Vineyards** *(860-535-1222)*, known for its Burgundian-style Chardonnay.

Whaling bark at Mystic Seaport

North of the vineyard, turn east on Conn. 184, then south on Conn. 2 to **Randall's Ordinary** *(860-599-4540)*. Almost everything served in this restaurant, housed in a 1680s farmhouse used on the Underground Railroad, is cooked over an open hearth. Ingredients are limited almost entirely to those available in the early 1700s.

Connecticut River Valley★

45 miles ● 1 to 2 days ● Spring through fall ● The many state parks along or near this route offer a variety of choices for picnics, hiking, and swimming.

Winding some 400 miles south from the Canadian border to Long Island Sound, the Connecticut River ends its long journey in the peaceful rolling hills of south-central Connecticut. This drive parallels the river's last few miles, taking in tranquil villages, an actor's castle, and a fanciful Victorian opera house.

We begin in Middletown, which straddles a bend in the river, and ramble south along the west bank as far as Essex. The route then veers north, crossing the Connecticut at Chester, and returning to Middletown along the east bank.

By the mid-1700s, shipbuilding and West Indies trade had made ❶ **Middletown** *(Greater Middlesex County Chamber of Commerce 860-347-6924),* located on the Connecticut River halfway between Hartford and Long Island Sound, the colony's wealthiest town. **Wesleyan University** was founded here in 1831. Among the town's variety of interesting attractions, the 1810 **General Mansfield House** *(151 Main St. 860-346-0746. Sun.-Mon. p.m.; adm. fee)* features changing exhibits culled from the Middlesex County Historical Society's extensive collection. Nearby, some of the area's finest handcrafts—including pottery, weaving, basketry, and jewelry—are displayed and sold at **Wesleyan Potters** *(350 S. Main St. 860-347-5925. Tues.-Sun.),* a 100-member cooperative guild. An excellent Judaica collection is on exhibit in **Adeth Israel Synagogue** *(48 Old Church Rd. 860-346-4709).* And finally, the steamed cheeseburgers at the landmark **O'Rourke's Diner** *(28 Main St. 860-346-6101)* may be an acquired taste, but the home-made soups and all-day breakfasts satisfy almost everyone.

Leaving town, the drive zips south on Conn. 9 to Conn. 154 toward Higganum. On this road, to the left, **Seven Falls** provides a picnic spot beside a series of cascading waterfalls.

Farther along at **Haddam Meadows State Park** *(860-345-8521),* representatives from several Native American tribes are among the participants who re-create American life between 1640 and 1840 at the annual **Quinnehtukqut Rendezvous and Native American Festival** *(860-282-1404. Third weekend in August; adm. fee).*

In **Haddam,** the gambrel-roofed 1794 **Thankful Arnold House** *(Hayden Hill and Walkley Hill Rds. 860-345-2400. July–Columbus Day p.m.; adm. fee),* with its superb period herb and vegetable gardens, was built on land purchased from the Wangonk tribe in the 1600s. The cemetery across the way dates from 1711.

Prominent in the 18th century as a shipbuilding town,

❷ Chester★

(Greater Middlesex County Chamber of Commerce 860-526-4598) now claims tourism as its major industry. Near tiny Main Street, lined with antique and gift shops, the **Wheat Market** *(4 Water St. 860-526-9347. Closed Sun.)* sells gourmet picnic fixings. If your timing is right, you can check out the **Chester Fair** the last weekend in August.

Farther south lies

Ship drawing at the Connecticut River Museum, Essex

Deep River, once home to George Read, a 19th-century founder of the local ivory industry and a strident abolitionist who sheltered runaway slaves along the Underground Rail-road. Give the kids time to browse at the **Great American Trading Company** *(39 Main St. 860-526-4335),* a warehouse

Fisherman on an Essex dock

full of wooden toys, puzzles, and almost everything else fun that's not made of plastic. The 1840 **Stone House** *(S. Main St. 860-526-5684. July-Aug. Sat.-Sun. p.m.; donations)* features locally manufactured goods, including ivory ware, Victorian furnishings, marine artifacts, and a piano carved from Hartford's Charter Oak. Felled in 1856, the oak hid the colony's charter during a troubled period in the late 1600s.

From Deep River, continue south to Centerbrook, taking a right onto Main Street. Main Street Centerbrook merges with Main Street **Ivoryton,** a tiny town where you'll find the headquarters of the **Hollycroft Foundation** *(Main St. 860-767-2624),* which hosts an internationally acclaimed sculpture exhibition each summer on 8 acres of woodland, marshland, and landscaped gardens. The nearby **Ivoryton Playhouse** *(103 Main St. 860-767-7318)* launched its first show in 1930. Summertime home of New York City's River Rep Company, the theater counts Katharine Hepburn and Marlon Brando among its noted alumni. Local groups perform year-round. Down the road, the **Museum of Fife & Drum** *(62 N. Main St. 860-767-2237. June-Aug. weekends; adm. fee)* traces the development of American martial music from the Revolutionary War to the present; free summer concerts are offered Tuesdays at 7:30 p.m.

Travel back through Centerbrook to Conn. 154 and follows signs to the **Valley Railroad Company** *(860-767-0103. Call for schedule; adm. fee).* Their sightseeing tour of the valley includes a jaunt on a luxurious, classic Pullman car, and a tour of the river aboard a southern-style steamboat. If you simply want a riverboat cruise, contact the Deep River Navigation Company *(806-526-4954)*.

The West Avenue exit off Conn. 154 leads to ❸ **Essex**★★, one of the valley's most charming towns and one of the region's most important shipbuilding centers in the 18th and 19th centuries. The sea captains' houses lining the town's winding streets have been joined by a myriad of antique shops and galleries.

At the foot of Main Street is **Steamboat Dock,** the site of New England's oldest continuously operating wharf (1640). It served as a stopping point for a turn-of-the-century steamboat service that ran between New York City and Hartford. Housed in a circa 1879 steamboat warehouse, the **Connecticut River Museum**★ *(67 Main St. 860-767-8269. Tues.-Sun.; adm. fee)* traces area history with ship models, prints, navigational tools, and paintings. A working reproduction of the first submarine, the 1775 *American Turtle*, is on display in one of the many galleries. The **Essex Art Association** *(10 N. Main St. 860-767-8996. Late April-Oct.)* exhibits and sells local artwork. If you're in need of refreshment, stop by the taproom at the historic **Griswold Inn** *(36 Main St. 860-767-1776),* described earlier in this century by bon vivant American journalist Lucius Beebe as one of the handsomest in America.

Leaving Essex, backtrack north on Conn. 154, then turn east on Conn. 148. The **Chester-Hadlyme Ferry** *(860-566-7635. April–mid-Dec.; fare),* which has been transporting vehicles across the Connecticut River for more than 200 years, will carry you, too. That wonderful, brooding fieldstone structure dominating the far cliff is ❹ **Gillette Castle**★★ located in **Gillette Castle State Park** *(67 River Road, E. Haddam. 860-526-2336. Daily Mem. Day–Columbus Day; weekends Columbus Day–late Dec.; adm. fee for castle, no fee for state park).* William Gillette, famous for his stage role as Sherlock Holmes, designed the 24-room fantasy to resemble those the estates along the Rhine River. Here he lived with his 15 cats from 1919 to 1937. His love of animals, gadgets, and craftsmanship is evident throughout the place.

After visiting the castle, and perhaps strolling along one of the park's trails, pick up Conn. 82 and follow signs to **East Haddam**★, home of the **Goodspeed Opera House**★★ *(860-873-8664. April-Dec.; adm. fee).* Saved from demolition in 1958 and restored to its 1876 Victorian

133

Moodus Noises

The area surrounding the little Connecticut River Valley town of Moodus has been haunted for ages by strange subterranean sounds, similar to rolling thunder or, at times, to a sharp cannon shot. Years will pass between incidents, but they must have been common enough when the Indians named this Machemoodus, or "place of noises." Today geologists associate the noises with shallow earthquakes.

splendor, it now presents productions of both musical classics and new works. Call ahead for information on tours, given on Mondays and Saturdays from June through October, which include the ladies' drinking parlor and dressing rooms. Lunch is served next door at the newly restored 1853 **Gelston House** *(860-873-1411. Wed.-Sun.)*.

In town behind St. Stephen's Church, you'll find the 1749 **Nathan Hale Schoolhouse** *(Main St. 860-873-9547. Mem. Day–Labor Day Sat.-Sun. p.m.; donations),* where the soon-to-be Revolutionary War hero spent a year as a schoolmaster from 1773 to 1774. Legend says the bell in the church belfry was cast in Spain in 815.

The drive continues north on Conn. 149, then south on Conn. 151 to the **Amasa Day House** *(Moodus Green. 860-873-8144. Late May–mid-Oct. Wed.-Sun. p.m.; adm. fee).* Three generations of Days have left family heirlooms, furnishings, and beautifully stencilled floors in this charming 1816 colonial. There's a museum in the barn.

Returning to Middletown via Conn. 151 and Conn. 66, you'll pass the ❺ **Sunrise Resort** *(Conn. 151. 860-495-6056),* host to four summer music festivals—Cajun and zydeco, Irish, traditional jazz, and bluegrass. Sit back and enjoy.

Goodspeed Opera House at dusk, East Haddam

Quiet Corner

100 miles ● 2 days ● Late spring through mid-autumn ● Peak foliage season is early to mid-October. Roads are less crowded than in other New England leaf-peeping areas.

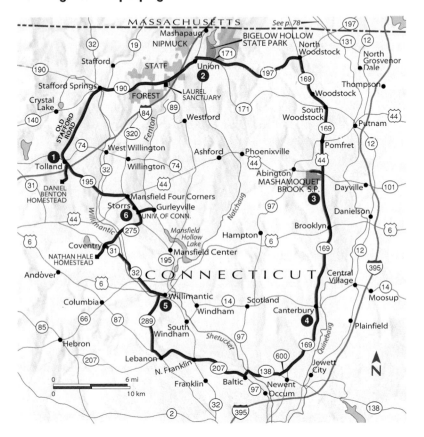

See p. 78

Connecticut's northeastern corner was overlooked for so long that only recently did anyone think to give it a name. The Quiet Corner appellation doesn't necessarily imply that the rest of the Nutmeg State is noisy; it's just that very little noise ever gets made about *this* region.

It's not as if the area was settled yesterday. One of the colonial post roads between New York and Boston passed this way, and substantial 18th-century houses grace the area villages. This route encounters the bustling University of Connecticut and a manufacturing town dating from New England's industrial heyday. But it also travels miles and miles of rambling country roads, threading together places that are nothing if not…quiet.

Quiet Corner

From Tolland, the route arcs north, then east through wooded countryside along the Massachusetts border. Continuing due south, it links a series of classic New England towns, each with a lovely green and steepled churches. Meandering back to Tolland, the drive visits his-toric mill towns and shrines to the American Revolution.

❶ Tolland *(Chamber of Commerce 860-872-0587)* is a village of white clapboard colonial houses enlivened by a few colorful Victorians facing its long town green. Settled in 1713, it was the 18th-century home of Ulysses S. Grant's ancestors. Preserved cells and tools of the trade comprise the **Tolland County Jail Museum** *(52 Tolland Green. 860-870-9599. Mid-May–mid-Oct. Sun. p.m.; donations),* located inside the 32-prisoner facility used as a jail from when it was built in 1856 to 1968. The 1893 warden's house, attached, now contains five exhibit rooms devoted to local history. Walk a block to the **Hicks-Stearns Museum** *(42 Tolland Green. 860-875-7552. Mid-May–mid-Oct. Sun. p.m.; adm. fee),* built in colonial times and Victorianized in the 1870s. Today it looks much as if its 19th-century occupants had just gone out for a stroll.

Two miles outside town, via Cider Mill and Metcalf Roads, stands the **Daniel Benton Homestead** *(860-872-8673. Mid-May–mid-Oct. Sun. p.m.; donations).* A splendidly

preserved New England Cape farmhouse, the old-est part dates from 1720. Much of the interior woodwork and even the window glass are original, as are the ghosts of Revo-lutionary War soldier Elisha Benton and his fiancée, said to haunt the place. American painter Thomas Hart Benton is descended from the Bentons who lived here.

Countryside near Canterbury

Traveling north from Tolland, take Old Stafford Road and Conn. 190 through Stafford Springs to **Laurel Sanctuary** on the grounds of Nipmuck State Forest. Pathways wind through a forest of laurel bushes—rising to a treelike 10 or 12 feet—that explode with pink and white blossoms in early summer.

Three miles ahead on Conn. 190, the tiny village of
❷ **Union** was among the last towns to be settled east of the
Connecticut River. Head east past scenic Bigelow Hollow
State Park to reach Conn. 169 at North Woodstock. Four
miles to the south is **Woodstock,** with its handsome town
common. The unmistakable jewel of domestic architecture
in the Quiet Corner rests opposite.

Built in 1846 for the influential merchant and abolitionist publisher Henry C. Bowen, **Roseland Cottage**★
*(556 Conn. 169. 860-928-4074. Mem. Day–Labor Day Wed.-
Sun.; Fri.-Sun. through mid-Oct.; adm. fee)* is Gothic Revival
in style, but also advertises the individuality of its owner.
The house is painted bright rose, after his favorite
flower, and the barn houses one of America's earliest
bowling alleys. Four Presidents enjoyed Bowen's hospi-
tality, and they would doubtless recognize Roseland's
sumptuous parlors today.

Bigelow Pond at Bigelow Hollow
State Park

137

Continue south on Conn. 169 and west on US 44 to
❸ **Mashamoquet Brook State Park** *(860-928-6121. Adm.
fee in season)* At the park entrance, the **Brayton Grist Mill
and Marcy Blacksmith Museum** *(Mem. Day–Labor Day
Sat.-Sun. p.m.)* chronicles the days of water-powered
milling and houses a collection of tools used for over 125
years by a local blacksmith family. The park's **Wolf Den
Trail** leads to the cave where Revolutionary War hero
Israel Putnam is said to have cornered and killed a wolf
that had been terrorizing the surrounding farms.

That same General Putnam is grandly memorialized
in the town of **Brooklyn,** 5 miles south after you rejoin
Conn. 169. Putnam, one of the American officers at the
Battle of Bunker Hill, is interred within the base of a
massive equestrian statue that stands by the roadside just
south of town center. Also related to Putnam history is
the gracious 1771 **Meeting House** facing the green.
When Putnam wasn't commanding armies or fighting
wolves, he served as sexton for the congregation here.

In nearby ❹ **Canterbury,** the **Prudence Crandall
Museum** *(Conn. 169 at Conn. 14. 860-546-9916. Feb.–mid-
Dec. Wed.-Sun.; adm. fee)* commemorates a different sort of
Connecticut hero. Prudence Crandall was a teacher who,
at the invitation of Canterbury's citizens in 1832, estab-
lished a school in this handsome 1805 federal house.
Later that year, she accepted a young black woman as a
student, and the town turned against her. When her

Monument to Maj. Gen. Israel
Putnam, Brooklyn

white students withdrew, she set up her academy "for the
reception of young Ladies and little Misses of Color."
Though she survived court challenges, she was hounded
from town by her hostile neighbors. (Half a century later,
the state legislature voted her an annuity.) The museum
houses permanent and changing exhibits, including three
period rooms on the first floor and an upstairs room
devoted to Crandall's Canterbury experiment.

South of Canterbury, drive west through Baltic to
sedate **Lebanon,** an unlikely center of Revolutionary War
activity. Unlikely—until you recall that in the 1770s, one
of the main roads connecting Boston with the middle
Atlantic colonies led right through town, along its mile-
long green. Facing the green are the **Governor Jonathan
Trumbull House** *(Mid-May–mid-Oct. Tues.-Sat. p.m.; adm.
fee),* built in 1740 in a chaste early Georgian style; and the
War Office *(Mid-May–mid-Oct. Sat.-Sun. p.m.; adm. fee),* a
little red gambrel-roofed structure dating from the 1720s.
Here, Governor Trumbull convened Connecticut's Council
of Safety to coordinate the state's war effort. George
Washington, Henry Knox, Israel Putnam, and the Marquis
de Lafayette all met with Trumbull within these walls.

A few miles north the swift Willimantic River provided
power for 19th-century textile mills in the small city of
❺ **Willimantic.** Here, the American Thread Company
once made the strong red thread that holds together
major league baseballs. (It still does, under a different
name, but like most textile firms it moved south long
ago.) The glory days of Willimantic industry are recalled
in the **Windham Textile & History Museum** *(Corner of
Union and Main Sts. 860-456-2178. Fri.-Sun.; adm. fee),*
housed in the Willimantic Linen Company's one-time
company store. The museum features re-creations of
rooms from a textile boss's 19th-century mansion, as well
as typical tenement quarters of the same era. On the top
floor, the Dunham Hall Library's polished beams soar
above the space where workers once studied—and
where some learned English—in their scant and precious
hours away from the job.

Coventry, northwest of Willimantic, is rich in associations with Connecticut's official state hero, Nathan Hale.
The young schoolmaster, whom the British hanged as a
Revolutionary War spy, was raised on the farm now preserved as the **Nathan Hale Homestead** *(2299 South St.*

860-742-6917. Mid-May–mid-Oct.; adm. fee). The big Georgian house looks much as it did in 1776, the year of Hale's death, when his boyhood home was rebuilt and enlarged. Inside, many Hale family possessions are gathered among period furnishings; outdoors, stone walls and maple trees look ready to welcome home those Hale brothers who did survive the war.

Just up the road, the **Strong-Porter House** *(South St. Mid-May–mid-Oct. Sat.-Sun. p.m.; adm. fee)* is a typical New England saltbox built and expanded over generations; Nathan Hale's great-uncle built the oldest portion about 1730. The grounds include a carpenter's shop, carriage shed, and exhibit barn.

The ❻ **Storrs** section of Mansfield is home to the **University of Connecticut,** which sprawls along either side of Conn. 195. For visitors, the main campus attractions are the **William Benton Museum of Art** *(860-486-4520. Tues.-Sun.),* which is particularly strong in 20th-century American art and design. Also of interest, the

Connecticut State Museum of Natural History *(Wilbur Cross Bldg. 860-486-4460. Thurs.-Mon. p.m.)* features exhibits on New England's Algonquian Indians and an extensive collection relating to the region's wildlife and ecology. Special Family and Discovery Day programs *(adm. fee)* focus on specific themes, using lectures, hands-on displays, and live demonstrations.

A quick drive just a quarter of a mile off campus via Gurleyville

Brick textile mill, once operated by American Thread Company, Willimantic

and Chaffeeville Roads will bring you to the **Gurleyville Grist Mill** *(860-429-6526. Late May–mid-Oct. Sun. p.m.).* This foursquare, early 1800s stone structure along the Fenton River is believed to be Connecticut's last surviving stone gristmill. A succession of mills have been built on the site, where colonists first began bringing their grain harvests in 1720.

90 miles ● 1 to 2 days ● Summer through fall ● Rush hour traffic can be heavy in and around Hartford.

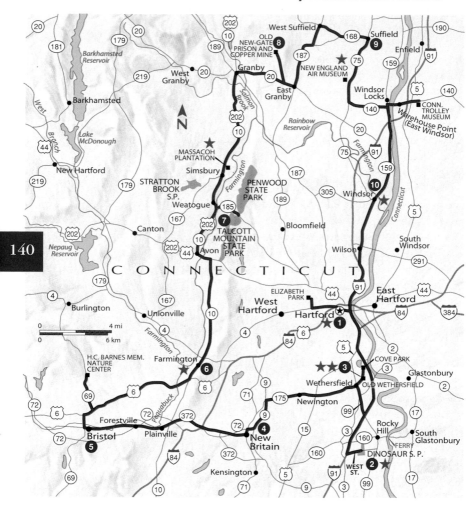

An unlikely outpost of tobacco cultivation and a cradle of American industry, this portion of the Connecticut River Valley contains a unique juxtaposition of urban and rural life. Shade tobacco, a variety prized by cigar manufacturers, grows perfectly in the valley's climate. The industry—clocks, tools, firearms—was the domain of the archetypal Connecticut Yankee written about by Hartford resident Samuel Langhorne Clemens.

From the capital of Hartford, the route heads west away from the valley toward the historic industrial centers of

New Britain and Bristol. Veering north, then east, it visits a skein of picture-perfect towns dating from colonial days, then returns to the capital city of Hartford along the Connecticut River's genteel west bank.

The English who settled **❶ Hartford**★ *(Convention and Visitors Bureau, One Civic Center Plaza. 860-728-6789 or 800-446-7811)* in 1635 supplemented their modest farming existence by trading corn, game, and eventually tobacco. (Today's settlers trade in insurance.) A walking tour brochure of downtown, available at the visitors bureau, covers 28 sights, including the following highlights:

The federal-style **Old State House** *(800 Main St. 860-522-6766),* designed by Charles Bulfinch in 1796, features a splendidly restored Senate chamber and a Gilbert Stuart portrait of George Washington. The **Wadsworth Atheneum**★★ *(600 Main St. 860-278-2670. Tues.-Sun.; adm. fee)* houses more than 45,000 objects, including an excellent collection of Hudson River school paintings, locally made Colt revolvers, and the Fleet Gallery of African-American Art. The 1782 **Butler-McCook Homestead** *(396 Main St. 860-522-1806. Mid-May–mid-Oct. Tues., Thurs., and Sun.; adm. fee),* occupied by descendants of the same family for 189 years, contains fine furnishings reflecting the changing tastes of several generations. Some 125 varieties of trees and a magnificently restored antique carousel (just 50 cents a ride) grace **Bushnell Park** *(Elm and Trinity Sts. 860-232-6710).* Rising above town, the gold-domed, marble-and-granite **Connecticut State Capitol** *(210 Capitol Ave. 860-240-0222. Mon.-Fri.),* designed by Gothic Revival master Richard M. Upjohn, gleams as a fine example of ornate, exuberantly confident Victorian public architecture.

Venture beyond the downtown region and visit the whimsically elaborate 19-room Picturesque Gothic mansion now known as the **Mark Twain House**★★ *(351 Farmington Ave. 860-493-6411. Closed Tues. Columbus Day–Mem. Day; adm. fee).* Samuel Langhorne Clemens built his house in 1874, and it was within the Louis Comfort Tiffany interiors—this country's only remaining Tiffany rooms open to public view—that he wrote the American classics *The Adventures of Tom*

Dome of the Old State House, Hartford

Sawyer and *Adventures of Huckleberry Finn.*

Next door, the **Harriet Beecher Stowe Center** *(71 Forest St. 860-525-9317. Closed Mon. Columbus Day–May; adm. fee)* honors the author of *Uncle Tom's Cabin,* who lived here from 1873 to 1896. Beautifully restored rooms feature Stowe's personal and professional belongings.

Late June is the best time to visit the **Elizabeth Park Rose Gardens** *(Prospect Ave. 860-722-6514),* when 14,000 rose bushes reach peak bloom. But there are also perennial and rock gardens, outdoor concerts, and winter ice skating. The greenhouses are open weekdays year-round.

South of Hartford off I-91, ❷ **Dinosaur State Park**★ *(400 West St., Rocky Hill. 860-529-8423. Exhibit center closed Mon.; adm. fee)* preserves beneath a geodesic dome 500 footprints left 200 million years ago by carnivorous dinosaurs. Exhibits include an 86-foot-long diorama of a Jurassic mudflat. To make your own cast of a dinosaur track, bring along cooking oil, cloth rags, paper towels, a 5-gallon plastic bucket, and 10 pounds of plaster of Paris. The outdoor casting center is open May through October.

Backtrack on I-91 and exit on Conn. 99 to the historic district of ❸ **Old Wethersfield**★★. Wethersfield, one of the state's oldest English settlements, dates back to 1634, when a group of English adventurers came to explore the region. Once home to a fine harbor, the town grew into an important colonial commercial center for the Connecticut River Valley. Its heritage is preserved in more than 115 historic houses built before 1850—comprising the state's largest historic district. Start at the **Visitor Center** *(200 Main St. 860-529-7161. Tues.-Sun.)* in the Keeney Memorial Cultural Center and pick up a walking tour map. For a good overview of town history, stop by the **Wethersfield Museum** at the same location.

Just up the street, the **Webb-Deane-Stevens Museum** ★★ *(211 Main St. 860-529-0612. May-Oct. Wed.-Mon., Nov.-April Sat.-Sun.; adm. fee)* encompasses three restored 18th-century houses. The 1752 **Webb House,** with its gambrel roof and wide center hall, is typical of a wealthy merchant's residence. Next door, the 1766 **Silas Deane House** belonged to a delegate of the First Continental Congress. And the 1788 Georgian **Isaac Stevens House,** which remained in the same family for 170 years, reflects the lifestyle of a middle-class family in the years following independence.

The hewn overhang, small casement windows, and

Early Insurance

Nowadays, Hartford is known as the Insurance City. Back in the days of the American frontier, the Connecticut capital was famous for another form of insurance—the Colt revolver. Samuel Colt, who designed the first practical firearm with a revolving cylinder mechanism, originally set up shop in 1836 in Paterson, New Jersey. A little over a decade later, Colt moved the business to his native Hartford (today it is in West Hartford). The ingenuity of this Connecticut Yankee gave rise to a popular saying in the Old West: "God made all men, but Colonel Colt made them equal."

142

simple design of the circa 1710 **Buttolph-Williams House** ★ *(249 Broad St. 860-247-8996. May-Oct. Wed.-Mon.; adm. fee)* reflect the austerity of the early settlers. Authentically furnished, the house also includes an impressive collection of woodenware in the kitchen.

During Old Wethersfield's maritime prime, traders stored products waiting to be shipped in places such as the circa 1690 **Cove Warehouse** *(860-529-7656. Mid-May–mid-Oct. Sat.-Sun.; donations)*, to the north of town at Cove Park.

❹ **New Britain** gained its Hardware City nickname

Webb-Deane-Stevens Museum in Old Wethersfield

because of its numerous metalworking industries. The downtown area is rich in art deco architecture, and a walking tour brochure is available at the Chamber of Commerce *(55 W. Main St. 860-229-1665)*.

Take some time and follow the development of American art from the 1740s to the present while perusing the more than 5,000 works at the **New Britain Museum of American Art** ★ *(56 Lexington St. 860-229-0257. Tues.-Sun.)*. John Singleton Copley, James Abbott McNeill Whistler, John Singer Sargent, Andrew Wyeth, and Georgia O'Keeffe are but a few of the artists represented. If the kids aren't satisfied with this museum's "hands on" alcove, take them over to the **New Britain Youth Museum** *(30 High St. 860-225-3020. Tues.-Sat.)*, which has lots of interactive exhibits exploring historical and cultural themes.

Follow Conn. 372 west to **⑤ Bristol** (*Chamber of Commerce 860-584-4718*). Dubbed the Cradle of the American Clock Industry, the city is home to the **American Clock & Watch Museum**★ (*100 Maple St. 860-583-6070. April-Nov.; adm. fee*). The sonorous ticking, whirling gears, and handsome countenances of more than 3,000 timepieces make this a good place to kill an hour.

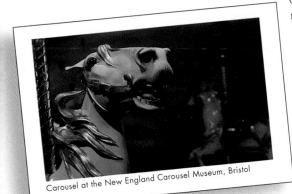

Carousel at the New England Carousel Museum, Bristol

Bristol also holds the delightful **New England Carousel Museum**★ (*95 Riverside Ave. 860-585-5411. Closed Mon. Nov.-March; adm. fee*), a fanciful assemblage of carousel pieces—mostly hand-carved—in various stages of restoration. A collection of miniature working carousels includes one made from 747 paper clips. To spend some time with live animals, visit the interpretive center and nature trails of the 70-acre **H.C. Barnes Memorial Nature Center** (*175 Shrub Rd. 860-589-6082. Wed.-Sun.*), a great place to stretch your legs and learn about the outdoors.

Head east on US 6 to the prosperous colonial town of **⑥ Farmington**★ and the wonderful **Hill-Stead Museum**★★ (*35 Mountain Rd. 860-677-9064. Tues.-Sun.; adm. fee*). Steel industrialist Alfred Atmore Pope's colonial revival house was designed around the turn of the century by his daughter, Theodate, in collaboration with McKim, Mead & White. Pope filled it with his extensive French Impressionist collection and loads of antiques. In a letter to Alfred's wife, American impressionist Mary Cassatt wrote: "Oh! You will enjoy your place. There's nothing like making pictures with real things." Indeed, Hill-Stead and its magnificent gardens, designed by Beatrix Farrand, provide artistic inspiration.

The 1720 **Stanley-Whitman House** (*37 High St. 860-677-9222. May-Oct. Wed.-Sun., Nov.-April Sun. only; adm. fee*) is a classic saltbox with exhibits and furnishings that interpret Farmington's early history. After stopping for a meal at the **Grist Mill Restaurant** (*44 Mill Lane. 860-676-8855*), located in a 350-year-old mill overlooking the Farmington River, wind north through the countryside to **Avon.** The 20 studios of the **Farmington Valley Arts Center** (*25 Arts Center Lane. 860-678-1867*) open to the public at various times, according to each artist's schedule. Within the center, the **Fisher Gallery and Shop** *(Closed Mon.-Tues. Jan.-Oct.)* sells the work of more than 300 artists.

Continue north to ❼ **Talcott Mountain State Park** *(860-242-1158. Tower and museum open mid-April–Aug. Thurs.-Sun. and daily Sept.-Oct.)*. Just after turning onto Conn. 185, watch for the **Pinchot Sycamore.** With a height of 93 feet and a crown spread of 138 feet, it's Connecticut's largest tree on record. At the park, a 1.5-mile trail leads to the mountaintop, a local history museum, and a fabulous view that's even better from the 165-foot **Heublein Tower.**

Back on U.S. 202/Conn. 10, the drive rambles farther north to the **Massacoh Plantation★** *(800 Hopmeadow St., Simsbury. 860-658-2500. Daily May-Oct.; adm. fee)*. Nine historic buildings filled with exhibits and staffed by costumed guides recall Simsbury's 300 years of history.

At Granby, take Conn. 20 east and follow signs for ❽ **Old New-Gate Prison and Copper Mine** *(Newgate Rd. 860-653-3563. Mid-May–Oct. Wed.-Sun.; adm. fee)*. North America's first chartered copper mine housed Loyalist sympathizers during the Revolutionary War. It then served as a state prison until 1827. After touring the aboveground ruins, explore the dank underground mine and cells where prisoners spent their miserable existence. Bring a sweater.

First Church, Windsor

As you drive back toward the Connecticut River, keep an eye out for tobacco fields and the long barns used to dry harvested leaves. In ❾ **Suffield** *(Chamber of Commerce 860-763-2396)* the 1761 **Hatheway House** *(55 S. Main St. 860-668-0055 or 247-8996. Mid-May–mid-Oct.; call for hours; adm. fee)* presents a fine example of 18th-century regional architecture. The north wing, added in 1794, is the area's earliest example of the neoclassical style. The interior retains its original French wallpaper and beautifully detailed plasterwork.

Follow Conn. 75 south to the **New England Air Museum★** *(Bradley International Airport, Windsor Locks. 860-623-3305. Adm. fee)*, the Northeast's largest aviation museum. More than 70 aircraft are on display, including military planes from World War I through Desert Storm. A cockpit simulator offers visitors a vicarious piloting experience.

Cross the Connecticut River into East Windsor on

Conn. 140 and hop aboard an antique streetcar at the **Connecticut Trolley Museum** *(58 North Rd. 860-627-6540. Daily Mem. Day–Labor Day, Labor Day–Mem. Day Sat.-Sun. only; adm. fee)* for a 3-mile ride through the countryside. The museum has more than 50 trolley cars dating from 1894 to 1949, and offers rides on several. Pay your fare and take as many trips as you wish.

Backtrack and head south to **⑩ Windsor★** *(Chamber of Commerce 860-688-5165)*, one of the state's oldest permanent English settlements and a leading tobacco grower. Among the antiques at the circa 1800 **Oliver Ellsworth Homestead** *(778 Palisado Ave. 860-688-8717. Mid-May–mid-Oct. Tues., Wed., and Sat.; adm. fee)*, is a Gobelin tapestry presented to Ellsworth by Napoleon Bonaparte. The **Windsor Historical Society** *(96 Palisado Ave. 860-688-3813. April-Oct. Tues.-Sat., Nov.-March Mon.-Fri.; adm. fee)* maintains two properties. The medical instruments and pharmaceutical recipes of a country doctor are displayed in the 1765 Georgian Colonial **Dr. Hezekiah Chaffee House,** made from locally fired bricks. Across the street stands the 1640 **Lt. Walter Fyler House,** one of the state's oldest surviving frame houses. It also contains the town's first post office and a general store. The society gives walking tours of the historic green by advance reservation.

View of the Tobacco Valley from East Granby

**180 miles ● 2 to 3 days ● Late spring through fall
● There aren't many overnight accommodations en
route, so reservations may be a good idea—
especially in foliage season.**

Tucked in the
northwestern corner of
the state, just hours
from the bustle of
New York City, the
Litchfield Hills are the
epitome of the pastoral
New England land-
scape. Wandering
the back roads of the
Housatonic Valley,
through picture-perfect
villages, it's hard
to imagine you're
anywhere else but
New England.

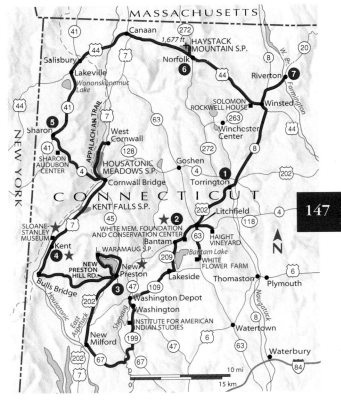

From the small city
of Torrington, this
quiet drive meanders
southwest through
serene Litchfield and
New Milford, then
turns north through a
flower-filled country-
side. Following along
the Housatonic River, it visits fine state parks, then arcs
from Salisbury to Norfolk before returning to Torrington
via a shrine to the American chair.

A 19th-century mill town and the birthplace of aboliti-
tionist John Brown, the city of ❶ **Torrington** is home of
the intricately designed, 17-room Victorian **Hotchkiss-
Fyler House★** *(192 Main St. 860-482-8260. April-Dec. Mon.-
Sat.; adm. fee).* Built between 1897 and 1900 by Orsamus
Fyler and bequeathed in 1956 to the Torrington Historical
Society by his daughter, Gertrude, the house remains just as
it was, with her furniture, antiques, and glass and porcelain
collections. Flowers, Gertrude's passion, abound—on
stenciling in the living room, in oil paintings by Connecticut
artists, even in glass baskets that take on the colors of a

floral bouquet. The interior is trimmed with a variety of fine carved hardwoods.

Head west to **Litchfield** *(Chamber of Commerce 860-482-6586)*, settled in 1719. Its appearance matches what many imagine as the ideal New England town, straight from central casting. The lovely village green, laid out in the early 1770s, marks the town center. The surrounding white colonial buildings form the core of the town's historic district—the first such designation in the state.

148

Litchfield shops

Follow in the footsteps of vice presidents Aaron Burr and John C. Calhoun, when they were students at the country's first law school. Now the **Tapping Reeve House and Law School** *(82 South St. 860-567-4501. Mid-May–mid-Oct. Tues.-Sun.; adm. fee)*, the 1773 structures exhibit student memorabilia and period furnishings. At the stately **Litchfield Historical Society Museum** *(7 South St. 860-567-4501. Mid-April–mid-Nov. Tues.-Sun.; adm. fee)*, seven galleries of exhibits trace the town's history from its earliest days through its golden age (1780-1840) and on to the present.

Two worthwhile stops just outside Litchfield will please your senses. Tours and tastings are offered throughout the day at the **Haight Vineyard** *(29 Chestnut Hill Rd. 860-567-4045)*, located east on Conn. 118. The state's first winery, opened in 1978, it grows five kinds of grapes and bottles eight different wines. South on Conn. 63, **White Flower Farm** *(860-567-8789. April-Dec.)* offers plants for sale as well as 4 acres of display gardens, at peak bloom from June through September.

From Litchfield, head west on US 202 to the ❷ **White Memorial Foundation and Conservation Center**★ *(71 Whitehall Rd. 860-567-0857. Adm. fee to museum)*. The privately owned wildlife sanctuary—the largest in the state—encompasses more than 4,000 acres of fields, waters, and woodlands. Find maps of the 35 miles of trails in the lobby of the nature museum, the foundation's educational arm. Visitors can rent bicycles in Litchfield at the Cycle Loft *(25 Litchfield Commons. 860-567-1713)* and ride on trails from the shop to the sanctuary.

At Bantam, Conn. 209 meanders south along the shoreline of **Bantam Lake,** Connecticut's largest natural lake. About 4 miles farther down, veer west toward **Lakeside** and watch for the immense sculpted elephant marking the entrance to the **Lorenz Studio and Gallery** *(226 Old Litchfield Rd. 860-567-4280).* Master glassblower and sculptor Larry LiVolsi displays his large glass-and-metal sculptures in an outdoor sculpture garden, while his more delicate pieces are preserved inside the barn gallery.

Turn south at the tiny town of Washington Depot to **Washington,** home of The Gunnery, an elite private school established in 1850. For antique furnishings and local historical artifacts, visit the **Gunn Memorial Library and Museum** *(5 Wykeham Rd. 860-868-7756. Thurs.-Sun.).* Then treat yourself to an elegant lunch in a lovely garden setting at the **Mayflower Inn** *(Conn. 47. 860-868-9466).*

South of Washington, Conn. 199 twists and turns 2.5 miles toward the **Institute for American Indian Studies** *(38 Curtis Rd. 860-868-0518. Closed Mon.-Tues. Jan.-March; adm. fee).* The modern museum tells the story of the Native American peoples who lived in the region before Europeans arrived. Their descendants are still here, and their personal reminiscences, recorded on tape against a background of traditional music and environmental sounds, provide meaningful insight into the artifacts and art on display. Outside, be sure to visit the authentically constructed Algonquian Village.

Follow Conn. 199 and Conn. 67 west to **New Milford,** and explore the quiet town via a walking tour of its historic homes and churches. Or take a leisurely stroll across the village green, one of Connecticut's largest.

Nearby ❸ **New Preston**★, on the East Aspetuck River, is a small, picturesque town packed with antique shops. Continue to the turnoff for **Lake Waramaug State Park** *(Lake Waramaug Rd. 860-868-2592. Adm. fee in summer),* which offers swimming and picknicking at one of the state's loveliest lakes. Looping around the lake, the route passes several country inns, including the **Inn on Lake Waramaug** *(North Shore Rd. 860-868-0563 or 800-LAKE-INN).*

Turkey Trot

On the Sunday before Thanksgiving, the **Inn at Lake Waramaug** *(New Preston. 800-LAKE-INN)* sponsors the Turkey Inn-Vitational. In a series of events—fastest eater, gymkhana, best dressed—turkeys from miles around go through their competitive paces. Lucky birds, these—"best dressed" means costume, not stuffing. The same pampered turkeys turn up year after year. So do about 300 turkey sports fans.

149

In summer, the inn's Boat House Cafe serves lunch overlooking the water. A bit farther along, **Hopkins Vineyard** *(Hopkins Rd. 860-868-7954. Daily May-Jan., Feb.-April Fri.-Sun. only)* offers free tastings of the wines made from the grapes grown here. Next door, the **Hopkins Inn** *(860-868-7295)* serves elegant meals with views of the lake.

New Preston Hill Road rambles west (changing names five times!) toward the New York border. As it meets US 7, look across the highway for the **Bulls Bridge Scenic Area.** Set in beautiful countryside and spanning the Housatonic River, the covered bridge is one of two in the state still open to cars. (The other stands just up the road in West Cornwall.)

Head north on US 7 to the upscale town of ❹ **Kent** ★ *(Chamber of Commerce 860-927-1463),* home to several private schools, myriad shops and art galleries, and many notable personages, including violinist Isaac Stern and former U.S. secretary of state Henry Kissinger. In the 1800s Kent was a workaday town, with three stone blast

Bulls Bridge over the Housatonic River

furnaces turning ore into iron. Recalling those years are the ruins of a blast furnace at the **Sloane-Stanley Museum and Kent Iron Furnace** ★ *(860-927-3849 or 566-3005. Mid-May–Oct. Wed.-Sun.; adm. fee),* north of town on US 7.

Artist Eric Sloane donated and arranged the museum's exhibit of early American tools to tell the story of America's craftsmanship heritage. He also used notations from an 1805 diary (on exhibit) to build a small cabin here. His studio in Warren, Connecticut, has been re-created in one wing of the museum.

It's possible to see the 200-foot-high cascading waterfall at **Kent Falls State Park** *(US 7. 860-927-3238. Parking fee weekends May–Oct.)* from the road. But take time for a closer look and stretch your legs along the staired pathway, which leads to the top of the waterfall.

Back on US 7, drive north beside the Housatonic River to **Housatonic Meadows State Park** *(860-927-3238. Mid-April–mid-Oct.)*, a popular spot for fly-fishing, picnicking, and hiking. For

Connecticut Agricultural Fair in Goshen

a short, scenic hike, continue just over a mile past the junction with Conn. 4 to the trailhead for the **Pine Knob Loop Trail,** which joins up with the Appalachian Trail.

A few miles farther north you can cross the bright red **West Cornwall Covered Bridge.** Incorporating a design patented by renowned architect Ithiel Town (1784-1844), the bridge has been in continuous use since its completion in 1864. A variety of artists and craftspeople sell their wares for reasonable prices at the **Cornwall Bridge Pottery Store** *(860-672-6545. Mem. Day-Christmas Wed.-Mon.; Jan.–Mem. Day Thurs.-Sun.)* on the other side of the bridge.

Backtrack on US 7 to the intersection with Conn. 4, and head west to the 684-acre **Sharon Audubon Center** *(325 Cornwall Bridge Rd. 860-364-0520. Adm. fee).* Eleven miles of trails wind through a varied terrain that includes forests, ponds, streams, fields, and marshland. An interpretive building houses a natural history museum and an adventure center for kids. Be sure to see the herb and wildflower gardens.

Turn north on Conn. 41 by the stone clock tower into the picturesque town of ❺ **Sharon.** Here the 1775 colonial **Gay-Hoyt House Museum** *(18 Main St. 860-364-5688. Mid-June–mid-Oct. Fri.-Sun.)* exhibits period furniture, antiques, paintings, and other historical items.

Continue past the prestigious Hotchkiss School to **Lakeville,** on the shores of Wononskopomuc Lake. The town, along with nearby Salisbury, once boasted the

Hot air balloon over rural Salisbury

country's most important iron mines and forges, which supplied cannon to the Continental Army during the Revolution. Kids love the **Salisbury Cannon Museum** *(15 Millerton Rd. Mem. Day–Sept. Sat.-Sun.)*, which focuses on local and regional history, especially the Revolutionary War period. The adjacent circa 1808 **Holley-Williams House** *(860-435-2878. Mem. Day–Sept. Sat.-Sun.; fee for tour)* displays 173 years of family furnishings and heirlooms.

Ready for a cuppa and a slice of tomato pie? Head up US 44 to **Salisbury** and the **Chaiwalla Tea Room** *(1 Main St. 860-435-9758. Daily Mem. Day–Labor Day; Wed.-Sun. rest of year)*. Owner Mary O'Brien, one of seven tea tasters appointed to the U.S. Board of Tea Experts, travels around the world to select her teas. Pick up a local trail guide at the tea room and walk off that tomato pie on one of the town's fine hiking trails—including 13 miles of the Appalachian Trail.

The drive continues east on US 44 through **Canaan,** and past the 1872 **Union Station,** believed to be this country's oldest railroad depot in continuous use. Then drive north on Conn. 272 to **Haystack Mountain State Park.** A half-mile trail leads to the mountain summit, where a 34-foot stone tower offers breathtaking views of

Long Island Sound, the Berkshires, and New York State.

In ❻ **Norfolk,** farther east on US 44, Yale University has been hosting its **Norfolk Chamber Music Festival**★★ *(Ellen Battell Stoeckel Estate. Summer 860-542-3000, Sept.-May 203-432-1966; adm. fee to concerts)* since 1941. From mid-June to mid-August, approximately four times a week, such groups as the Tokyo String Quartet and the New York Woodwind Quintet give concerts in the enclosed shed on the estate grounds. Seats are limited, so call well in advance for tickets. Concerts continue through early November as part of the Indian Summer Series.

On the outskirts of Winsted, Conn. 263 (Lake St.) leads west to the **Solomon Rockwell House** *(225 Prospect St. 860-379-8433. Mid-June–mid-Oct. Thurs.-Sun.),* an imposing 1813 Greek Revival home. Now owned by the Winchester Historical Society, the house is a repository for objects of local historical and cultural interest. Highlights include historical works by painter Erastus Salisbury Field and an extensive collection of Civil War memorabilia.

From Winsted, turn north on Conn. 8 then east on Conn. 20 to tiny, historic ❼ **Riverton.** In 1826 Lambert Hitchcock built a mill here to manufacture his now-famous chairs, many are on display in the **Hitchcock Museum**★ *(1 Robersville Rd. 860-738-4950. Mid-April–mid-Dec. Wed.-Sun.).* Hanging from the walls of the circa 1829 Gothic stone church, the ornate and intricately decorated chairs have an almost sculptural beauty. Other 18th- and early 19th-century chairs are also on exhibit, along with assorted antique painted furniture. The

Exhibits at the Hitchcock Museum, Riverton

Hitchcock Chair Company Factory Store *(Conn. 20. 860-379-4826),* in Lambert Hitchcock's original chair factory, sells both first- and second-quality pieces.

For a bite to eat, stop by the **Old Riverton Inn** *(Conn. 20. 860-379-8678. Wed.-Sun.).* Built in 1796 as a stagecoach stop, it serves lunch daily.

New England coastal view: Marblehead Harbor, Massachusetts

MAINE

Maine Publicity Bureau *800-533-9595.* General information, fall foliage and cross-country skiing updates.

Acadia National Park General information *207-288-3338.* Campground reservations *800-365-2267.*

Bureau of Parks and Lands *207-287-3821.* State park information.

Department of Inland Fisheries *207-287-2571.* Fishing and hunting regulations.

Department of Transportation road conditions *207-287-3427.*

Bed & Breakfast Down East, Ltd. *207-338-9764.* B&B reservation service.

NEW HAMPSHIRE

New Hampshire Office of Travel and Tourism *603-271-2666* or *800-258-3608.* General information, fall foliage updates (Sept.- Oct.), and special events information including antique and craft shows, festivals, and historical reenactments.

Department of Fish and Game *603-271-2743.* Hunting and fishing license information.

Division of Parks and Recreation *603-271-2665.* State parks information.

State Police *603-271-6900.* Weather and road conditions.

White Mountain National Forest General information *603-528-8721.* Campground reservations *800-280-2267.*

Bed & Breakfast Inns of New England *603-279-8348.* B&B listings and reservation service.

New Hampshire Room Reservations *800-ENJOY-NH.* B&B listings and reservation service.

VERMONT

Vermont Travel and Tourism General information *800-VERMONT.* Fall foliage updates (Sept.-Oct.) *802-828-3239.*

Agency of Natural Resources *802-241-3655.* State parks information.

Department of Forests, Parks and Recreation *802-244-8711.* Recreation information.

Green Mountain National Forest *802-747-6700.* General information.

Ski Conditions *802-229-0531* (Nov.-April)

State Police road conditions *802-828-4894* or *800-ICY-ROAD* (winter only)

The American Country Collection *518-370-4948.* B&B listings and reservation service.

MASSACHUSETTS

Massachusetts Office of Travel and Tourism *617-727-3201 or 800-227-MASS.* General information, seasonal calendar of events, fall foliage and skiing updates.

Department of Transportation road conditions *617-374-1234.*

Sportfishing Promotion Council *800-ASK-FISH.* Fishing license information.

A Bed & Breakfast Agency of Boston, Inc. *800-CITY-BNB.* B&B reservation service for Boston.

RHODE ISLAND

Rhode Island Tourism Division *800-556-2484.* General information and fall foliage updates.

Department of Environmental Management Fishing and hunting regulations *401-277-3075.* State parks information *401-277-2635.*

Bed and Breakfasts of Newport, Ltd. *800-800-8765.* B&B listings and reservations for the Newport area.

Bed and Breakfasts of Rhode Island *800-828-0000.* B&B listings and reservations for Rhode Island and the rest of New England.

CONNECTICUT

Connecticut Department of Tourism *800-CT-BOUND.* General information and fall foliage updates.

Department of Environmental Protection Hunting and fishing licenses *860-424-3105.* State parks information *860-424-3200.*

Department of Transportation
860-594-2650 or *800-443-6817*
(recorded message). Road conditions.
Bed and Breakfast, Ltd.
203-469-3260. B&B listings and
reservation service.
Covered Bridge *203-542-5944.*
B&B listings and reservation service.
Nutmeg Bed and Breakfast Agency
203-236-6698. B&B listings and
reservation service.

HOTEL & MOTEL CHAINS
(Accommodations in all six states unless otherwise noted)

Best Western International *800-528-1234*
Budget Host *800-BUD HOST* (Me., Mass.,
    and R.I. only)
Choice Hotels *800-4-CHOICE*
Clarion Hotels *800-CLARION*
Comfort Inns *800-228-5150*
Days Inn *800-325-2525*
Doubletree Hotels and Guest Suites
    800-222-TREE (Mass. and R.I. only)
Econo Lodge *800-446-6900* (Except R.I.)
Embassy Suites *800-362-2779* (Me. and
    Mass. only)
Fairfield Inn by Marriott *800-228-2800*
Friendship Inns Hotel *800-453-4511*
    (Except R.I.)
Hampton Inn *800-HAMPTON* (Except R.I.)
Hilton Hotels *800-HILTONS* (Mass. and
    Conn. only)
Holiday Inns *800-HOLIDAY*
Howard Johnson *800-654-2000*
LRI Loews Hotels *800-223-0888* (Except
    Vt. and Me.)
Motel 6 *800-466-8356*
Quality Inns-Hotels-Suites *800-228-5151*
Radisson Hotels Intl. *800-333-3333*
Ramada Inns *800-2-RAMADA* (Except N.H.)
Red Roof Inns *800-843-7663* (Vt., Mass., and
    Conn. only)
Ritz-Carlton *800-241-3333* (Mass. only)
Sheraton Hotels & Inns *800-325-3535*
Super 8 Motels *800-843-1991*
Travelodge International, Inc.
    800-255-3050 (Vt. and Mass. only)
Utell International *800-223-9868*
Westin Hotels and Resorts
    800-228-3000 (Mass. and R.I. only)

ILLUSTRATIONS CREDITS
Cover: James Randklev

Shawn G. Henry photographed Maine,
New Hampshire, and Vermont except
for the following pages: 20 Michael
Melford; 31 Bill Ballenberg; 44 José Azel;
46 Medford Taylor; 51 Ken Sherman.

Vincent J. Musi photographed Massa-
chusetts, Connecticut, and Rhode Island
except for the following pages: 85
Sarah Leen; 104 Michael Schwarz; 108
Annie Griffiths Belt; 109 James P. Blair;
111 Bob Sacha; 118 Ira Block; 148 Scott
Goldsmith; 151 Scott Goldsmith; 154-155
Steve Dunwell/The Image Bank.

NOTES ON AUTHORS AND PHOTOGRAPHERS

157

KAY AND WILLIAM G. SCHELLER have each
spent more than 25 years exploring
New England. A Massachusetts native,
Kay has contributed to and co-authored
numerous travel guides. Bill is a widely
published travel writer and a contributing editor to NATIONAL GEOGRAPHIC
TRAVELER. The Schellers live in northern
Vermont with their son, David.

Freelance photographer SHAWN G. HENRY
is as at home in Addis Ababa, Ethiopia,
and Phnom Penh, Cambodia, as he is in
Rangeley, Maine. His assignments for
the National Geographic Society have
extended from the eruption of Mount
Pinatubo in the Philippines to puffins in
Maine. When not traveling, Henry can
usually be found in late afternoon walking his dog, Ruby, in Raven Woods Park
in Gloucester, Massachusetts.

VINCENT J. MUSI logged over 8,000 miles
in New England on this freelance
photography assignment. His work for
newspapers, magazines, and books
has taken him around the United States
and abroad, but he is most comfortable
with a fly rod in hand and trout-bearing
water at his feet.

Index

*A*cadia N.P., Me. 19, 20
Adams N.H.S., Quincy, Mass. 98-99
Amherst, Mass. 76-77
Arlington, Vt. 60
Ashfield, Mass. 74
Augusta, Me. 27
Avon, Conn. 144-145

*B*angor, Me. 10-11
Bar Harbor, Me. 19
Barnstable, Mass. 108
Barre, Vt. 53
Bash Bish Falls, Mass. 66
Bath, Me. 15
Baxter S.P., Me. 12
Beauport, Gloucester, Mass. 95
Beavertail S.P., R.I. 119
Bellows Falls, Vt. 63
Bennington, Vt. 59-60
Berkshire Museum, Pittsfield, Mass. 68
Bethel, Me. 24-25
Billings Farm & Museum, Woodstock, Vt. 56
Blackstone River Valley National Heritage Corridor, Mass. 80-81
Blithewold Mansion and Gardens, Bristol, R.I. 116
Block Island, R.I. 119, 121
Blue Hill, Me. 19
Boothbay Harbor, Me. 16
Boston, Mass. 84-87
Brandon, Vt. 57
Branford, Conn. 123
Brattleboro, Vt. 63
Brewster, Mass. 109
Brimfield, Mass. 82
Bristol, Conn. 144
Bristol, R.I. 116
Brooklyn, Conn. 137
Brownington, Vt. 52
Brunswick, Me. 14-15
Bryant Pond, Me. 24
Burlington, Vt. 48-50

*C*ambridge, Mass. 87
Camden Hills S.P., Me. 17-18
Camden, Me. 17
Canaan, Conn. 152
Canterbury, Conn. 137-138
Canterbury Shaker Village, N.H. 35-36
Cape Cod National Seashore 110
Cape Porpoise, Me. 29

Castine, Me. 18
Castle in the Clouds, N.H. 42-43
Cathedral of the Pines, N.H. 37-38
Center Sandwich, N.H. 43
Charlestown, R.I. 121
Chatham, Mass. 111-112
Chester, Conn. 131
Chester, Vt. 62-63
Chesterfield Gorge, Mass. 74
Chesterwood, Stockbridge, Mass. 65
Chesuncook Village, Me. 11
Children's Museum, Boston, Mass. 86
Christa McAuliffe Planetarium, near Concord, N.H. 35
Cohasset, Mass. 101
Computer Museum, Boston, Mass. 86
Concord, Mass. 88-89
Concord, N.H. 35
Connecticut River Museum, Essex, Conn. 133
Conway, Mass. 75
Cornish-Windsor Covered Bridge, N.H.-Vt. 36, 55
Coventry, Conn. 138-139
Craftsbury, Vt. 51
Crawford Notch S.P., N.H. 47
Cummington, Mass. 74
Currier Gallery of Art, Manchester, N.H. 39

*D*artmouth College 36
Deep River, Conn. 131-132
Dennis, Mass. 109
Dinosaur S.P., Conn. 142
Dover, N.H. 33
Duxbury, Mass. 102

*E*ast Haddam, Conn. 133-134
East Haven, Conn. 123
East Windsor, Conn. 145-146
Ellacoya S.P., N.H. 42
Elmore S.P., Vt. 51
Equinox Sky Line Drive, Vt. 60-61
Essex, Conn. 133
Essex, Mass. 96
Exeter, N.H. 33

*F*all River, Mass. 105
Falmouth, Mass. 113
Farmington, Conn. 144
Farnsworth Art Museum,

Rockland, Me. 17
Fisher Museum of Forestry, Petersham, Mass. 83
Florence Griswold Museum, Old Lyme, Conn. 126
Fort Adams S.P., R.I. 118-119
Fort at No. 4, N.H. 37
Fort Knox S.P., Me. 18
Fort McClary S.H.S., Me. 30-31
Franconia, N.H. 44-45
Franconia Notch S.P., N.H. 45
Freedom Trail, Boston, Mass. 85
Freeport, Me. 27
Frost Place, Franconia, N.H. 44-45
Fruitlands Museums, Harvard, Mass. 90

*G*alilee, R.I. 120-121
Gilbertville, Mass. 82
Gillette Castle S.P., Conn. 133
Gloucester, Mass. 95
Goodspeed Opera House, East Haddam, Conn. 133-134
Grafton, Mass. 80
Grafton Notch S.P., Me. 25
Grafton, Vt. 63
Great Barrington, Mass. 66
Greenville, Me. 11-12
Groton, Conn. 128
Guilford, Conn. 124
Gulf Hagas, Me. 13
Gunstock Recreation Area, N.H. 42

*H*addam, Conn. 131
Haddam Meadows S.P., Conn. 131
Hammonasset Beach S.P., Conn. 125
Hammond Castle, Mass. 95
Hancock Shaker Village, Mass. 65
Hanover, N.H. 36
Hardwick, Mass. 82
Harkness Memorial S.P., Conn. 127
Harrisville, N.H. 38
Hartford, Conn. 141-142
Harvard, Mass. 90
Harvard University, Mass. 87
Henry Whitfield State Museum, Guilford, Conn. 124
Heritage New Hampshire, Glen, N.H. 46
Higgins Armory Museum, Worcester, Mass. 79
Hildene, Manchester, Vt. 61
Hill-Stead Museum, Farmington, Conn. 144
Hingham, Mass. 99-100

Historic Deerfield, Mass. 75
Hitchcock Museum, Riverton, Conn. 153
Holyoke, Mass. 77
Hotchkiss-Fyler House, Torrington, Conn. 147-148
Housatonic Meadows S.P., Conn. 151
House of the Seven Gables, Salem, Mass. 93
Hull, Mass. 100
Hyannis, Mass. 112

*I*pswich, Mass. 96
Isabella Stewart Gardner Museum, Boston, Mass. 86-87
Isles of Shoals, Me.-N.H. 32
Ivoryton, Conn. 132

*J*affrey Center, N.H. 38
Jamestown, R.I. 119
Jericho, Vt. 50
John Brown House, Providence, R.I. 115

*K*ancamagus Highway, N.H. 45-46
Katahdin Iron Works, Me. 13
Keene, N.H. 37
Kennebunk, Me. 29
Kennebunkport, Me. 29
Kent, Conn. 150
Kineo, Mount, Me. 12
Kingfield, Me. 26
Kokadjo, Me. 12

*L*ake Champlain Maritime Museum, near Vergennes, Vt. 57
Lake Sunapee, N.H. 36
Lake Waramaug S.P., Conn. 149-150
Lakeville, Conn. 151-152
Lawrence, Mass. 91
Lebanon, Conn. 138
Lenox, Mass. 67
Lexington, Mass. 87-88
Litchfield, Conn. 148-149
Lowell, Mass. 90, 91
Lubec, Me. 21
Lyman Allyn Art Museum, New London, Conn. 128

adison, Conn. 124-125

Maine Maritime Museum, Bath 15
Maine State Museum, Augusta 27
Manchester, N.H. 39
Manchester, Vt. 61
Mansfield, Mount, Vt. 50
Marblehead, Mass. 94
Mark Twain House, Hartford, Conn. 141-142
Martha's Vineyard, Mass. 113
Mashamoquet Brook S.P., Conn. 137
Meredith, N.H. 41
Middlebury, Vt. 57-58
Middletown, Conn. 130-131
Minute Man N.H.P., Mass. 88
Monadnock S.P., N.H. 38
Monhegan Island, Me. 17
Montpelier, Vt. 53
Moosehead Lake, Me. 11
Mount Greylock S.R., Mass. 68-69
Mount Holyoke College, South Hadley, Mass. 77
Mount Independence, Vt. 57
Mount Lebanon Shaker Village, Mount Lebanon, N.Y. 65
The Mount, near Lenox, Mass. 67
Mount Sunapee S.P., N.H. 36
Mount Tom S.R., Mass. 72
Mount Washington Cog Railway, N.H. 47
Museum of Fine Arts, Boston, Mass. 86
Museum of Science, Boston, Mass. 87
Mystic, Conn. 128-129

*N*aismith Memorial Basketball Hall of Fame, Springfield, Mass. 71-72
Nantucket, Mass. 111, 113
Naples, Me. 24
Narragansett, R.I. 120
Naumkeag, Stockbridge, Mass. 66
New Bedford, Mass. 104-105
New Britain, Conn. 143-144
New Castle, N.H. 32
New England Air Museum, Windsor Locks, Conn. 145
New England Aquarium, Boston, Mass. 86
New England Carousel Museum, Bristol, Conn. 144
New Hampshire Farm Museum, Milton, N.H. 42
New Haven, Conn. 122-123, 127
New London, Conn. 127-128

New Preston, Conn. 149-150
Newburyport, Mass. 97
Newport, R.I. 117-119
Nickels-Sortwell House, Wiscasset, Me. 15-16
Nickerson S.P., Mass. 109
Norfolk, Conn. 153
Norlands Living History Center Me. 26-27
Norman Rockwell Museum at Stockbridge, Mass. 65
North Adams, Mass. 69
North Conway, N.H. 46
North Oxford, Mass. 79-80
Northampton, Mass. 72-73

*O*gunquit, Me. 30
Old Fort Western, Augusta, Me. 27
Old Lyme, Conn. 126
Old Saybrook, Conn. 126, 127
Old Sturbridge Village, Mass. 81-82
Old Town, Me. 13
Old Wethersfield, Conn. 142-14
Orleans, Mass. 109-110, 111
Orono, Me. 13
Owls Head Transportation Museum, Owls Head, Me. 17
Oxford, Mass. 80

*P*arker River N.W.R., Mass. 97
Patten, Me. 13
Pawtucket, R.I. 116
Peabody Essex Museum, Salen Mass. 93-94
Penobscot Marine Museum, Searsport, Me. 18
Peterborough, N.H. 38-39
Petersham, Mass. 83
Pittsfield, Mass. 68
Plimoth Plantation, Mass. 103-104
Plymouth, Mass. 102-104
Plymouth, N.H. 41
Plymouth Notch Historic District, Plymouth Notch, Vt. 56
Polar Caves Park, N.H. 41
Portland, Me. 23-24
Portsmouth, N.H. 31-32
Portsmouth, R.I. 117
Providence, R.I. 114-116
Provincetown, Mass. 111
Purgatory Chasm S.R., Mass. 8(
Putney, Vt. 63

Index

Quabbin Reservoir, Mass. 82-83
Quechee Gorge, Vt. 55
Quincy, Mass. 98-99
Quoddy Head S.P., Me. 21

Rangeley Lake S.P., Me. 26
Rhododendron S.P., N.H. 37
Riverton, Conn. 153
Rockland, Me. 17
Rockport, Mass. 96
Roosevelt Campobello International Park, New Brunswick, Canada 21
Roseland Cottage, Woodstock Conn. 137
Ruggles House, Columbia Falls, Me. 20

Sagamore, Mass. 107
Saint Croix Island, Me. 21
St. Johnsbury, Vt. 52-53
Saint-Gaudens N.H.S., N.H. 36
Salem, Mass. 93-94
Salisbury, Conn. 151-152
Sandwich, Mass. 107-108
Schoodic Peninsula, Me. 20
Science Center of New Hampshire, Holderness, N.H. 43
Scituate, Mass. 101
Searsport, Me. 18
Sebago Lake S.P., Me. 24
Sharon, Conn. 151
Sheffield, Mass. 67
Shelburne Falls, Mass. 75
Shelburne Farms, Vt. 50
Shelburne Museum, Vt. 50
Skolfield-Whittier House, Brunswick, Me. 15
Slater Mill H.S., Pawtucket, R.I. 116
Smith College, Northampton, Mass. 72-73
Smugglers Notch, Vt. 50
South Berwick, Me. 33
South Hadley, Mass. 77
Southwest Harbor, Me. 20
Springfield, Mass. 71-72
Squam Lake, N.H. 43
Stanley Museum, Kingfield, Me. 26
Sterling and Francine Clark Art Institute, Williamstown, Mass. 64
Stockbridge, Mass. 65-66
Stonington, Conn. 127, 129
Stonington, Me. 18
Stony Creek, Conn. 123-124
Storrs, Conn. 139

Stowe, Vt. 51
Strawbery Banke Museum, Portsmouth, N.H. 30, 31
Submarine Force Museum, Groton, Conn. 128

Talcott Mountain S.P., Conn. 145
Tamworth, N.H. 43
Tanglewood, Lenox, Mass. 67
Texas Falls Recreation Area, Vt. 58
The Thimbles, Conn. 123-124
Thomaston, Me. 16
Tolland, Conn. 136
Torrington, Conn. 147-148

Uxbridge, Mass. 80-81

Wadsworth Atheneum, Hartford, Conn. 141
Walden Pond, Mass. 89-90
Waldoboro, Me. 16
Wareham, Mass. 104
Washington, Conn. 149
Watch Hill, R.I. 121
Wayside Inn, S. Sudbury, Mass. 90
Webb-Deane-Stevens Museum, Wethersfield, Conn. 142
Webster, Mass. 81
Weirs Beach, N.H. 41
Wells, Me. 30
Wells National Estuarine Research Reserve, Me. 30
Wentworth Coolidge Mansion, New Castle, N.H. 32
West Cornwall, Conn. 151
Westbrook, Conn. 125
Westfield, Mass. 72
Weston, Vt. 61-62
Weymouth, Mass. 99
White Memorial Foundation

and Conservation Center, near Litchfield, Conn. 148-149
White River Junction, Vt. 55
Wickford, R.I. 119-120
Wilhelm Reich Museum, Rangeley, Me. 26
Willard House and Clock Museum, Grafton, Mass. 80
William Cullen Bryant Homestead, Cummington, Mass. 74
Williamsburg, Mass. 73
Williamstown, Mass. 64-65
Willimantic, Conn. 138
Windsor, Conn. 146
Windsor, Vt. 55
Winslow House, Marshfield, Mass. 101
Wiscasset, Me. 15-16
Wolfeboro, N.H. 42
Wolfe's Neck Woods S.P., Me. 27
Woodman Institute, Dover, N.H. 33
Woods Hole, Mass. 113
Woodstock, Conn. 137
Woodstock, Vt. 56
Worcester, Mass. 79
World's End Reservation, Mass. 100

Yale University, Conn. 122-123
Yarmouth Port, Mass. 108-109
York Village, Me. 30

Zimmerman House, Manchester, N.H. 39

Composition for this book by the National Geographic Society Book Division. Printed and bound by R.R. Donnelly & Sons, Willard, Ohio. Color separations by Digital Color Image, Pensauken, New Jersey. Paper by Consolidated/Alling & Cory, WillowGrove, Pennsylvania. Cover printed by Miken Companies, Inc. Cheektowaga, New York.

Library of Congress Cataloging-in-Publication Data

Scheller , Kay.
  National Geographic's driving guides to America. New England / by Kay and William G. Scheller ; photographed by Shawn G. Henry and Vincent J. Musi ; prepared by the Book Division, National Geographic Society.
    p.   cm.
  Includes bibliographical references and index.
  ISBN 0-7922-3423-5. — ISBN 0-7922-3424-3
  1. New England — Tours. 2. Automobile travel — New England — Guidebooks.   I. Scheller, William.   II. Henry, Shawn G.
III. Musi, Vincent J.   IV. National Geographic Society (U.S.).   Book Division.   V. Title.
F2.3.S34   1996
917.404'43—dc20   96-24771
                                                              CIP

Visit the Society's Web site at http://www.nationalgeographic.com or GO NATIONAL GEOGRAPHIC on CompuServe.